In May 2012 Ron Luce, the founder of Teen Mania and my friend for almost two decades, was scheduled to preach at an area-wide crusade at Rose Stadium in Tyler, Texas. The night before he was to speak, we received the shocking news that his daughter and other Teen Mania staff members had been involved in a tragic plane crash. I recall as hundreds of people gathered on the football field that evening, joining hands to cry out to God for Ron and his family.

His book *Resilient* describes his journey through this time of personal testing. Ron sets aside all the shallow faith clichés we've heard all of our lives. This powerful book is a call to replace a theology of complacent faith with the power of resilient faith. I encourage you to read it and let it become truth that will set you free.

—Dr. David O. Dykes
Pastor, Green Acres Church, Tyler, Texas

I've seen, personally, the impact that Ron Luce has had as I was an invited guest to speak to over seventy thousand teens at his stadium events for teens several times. In this book, *Resilient*, Ron inspires both young and old to build a foundation of faith to bounce back no matter what life throws at us. A must-read!

—John C. Maxwell
Author and speaker
Founder, the John Maxwell Company and EQUIP Inc.

Finally! The church has been waiting for a book that calls Jesus followers to a rugged, radical faith. In an hour when counting the cost is no longer en vogue, Luce challenges disciples of Christ to seize the day, stay the course, run the race, and pay the price. The stories and testimonies will inspire you; the teaching will stretch you. But before you lay *Resilient* down, your spirit will cry, "Here am I; send me."

—Jeff Farmer
Chairperson, Pentecostal/Charismatic Churches
of North America

Resilient is much more than a book or a compelling testimony. This narrative serves as a biblically based, Christ-centered prescription for anyone who has ever confronted tumultuous circumstances. This book empowers the reader not just to survive but to thrive in the midst of life's storms. It's not just a must-read, it's a "must-do"!

—Rev. Samuel Rodriguez
President, NHCLC (Hispanic Evangelical Association)

Ron Luce has given a vital corrective to the faulty thinking and faulty presentations that have plagued too much of our Christian witness. Christ's clear directive to His followers was to produce more ardent followers—those whose loyalty to Him would be absolute—among all peoples and nations.

P9-CEJ-759

This landmark book serves as a plumb line pointing us back to true New Testament faith and discipleship.

—DAVID SHIBLEY
FOUNDER AND WORLD REPRESENTATIVE, GLOBAL ADVANCE

Contemporary Christians frequently transform the Bible into a narcissistic book. God's promises are construed into virtual guarantees for our well-being, health, finances, and families. But what happens when life throws us a major curve, something that does not fit into our comfortable, self-serving belief about the constant blessings of God? Ron Luce knows about that journey, from a self-satisfied Christian to a believer who has been tested by crisis and is resolved to finish well. Ron believes the key ingredient in this transformation is resilience. Where does one find or discover resilience? In this book Ron invites you to join him in search of secrets to resilience.

—RANDALL A. BACH
PRESIDENT, OPEN BIBLE CHURCHES

Christian rhetoric is filled with clichés. These trite platitudes become polite repartee when life's events are incomprehensible or painful to contemplate. Ron Luce takes us into his own personal journey by ripping back the curtains of cute phrases, revealing the agony of personal pain and the triumph of resilient faith in Jesus Christ. Ron continues his fight for future generations, showing how it will be a resilient faith that captures their hearts and gives them strength to stand the trials of life. I need resilient faith; you need resilient faith. Read *Resilient*, then live with resilient faith.

—CHARLES G. SCOTT
GENERAL BISHOP, PENTECOSTAL CHURCH OF GOD,
AUTHOR, *STORMS DON'T BOTHER ME*

How many times have I told someone I didn't know what they were going through, but Jesus does? Ron Luce speaks with authority as having his resilience tested and tried. But *Resilient* is not about the author. It's about you! In it you will find the profound truths of finishing well for God. Ron strips away the veneer of many modern Christian forms to reveal true Christianity and discipleship. Finishing well is more about beginning well with the right disciplines in our daily walk. When reading *Resilient,* with its brilliant life-to-truth examples, you will cry some, but then you will be inspired.

—CLYDE M. HUGHES
GENERAL OVERSEER, INTERNATIONAL PENTECOSTAL CHURCH OF CHRIST

In *Resilient* Ron Luce sounds a clarion call for authentic Christianity that grips real faith in unreal circumstances. His passionate challenge comes from the perspective of personal tragedy and a Spirit-empowered strength to persevere. A must-read!

—GORDON MCDONALD
GENERAL SUPERINTENDENT, PENTECOSTAL HOLINESS CHURCH OF CANADA

It is not uncommon for us to face circumstances in life that cause us to evaluate our core understandings of our relationship with God. In 2012, as the result of a tragic plane crash, the Luce family faced such an experience. In *Resilient* Ron Luce takes us back to the true depth and beauty of a relationship with Jesus that demands passionate commitment, disciplined pursuit and an unwavering faith in the One who allows us to persevere. No platitudes or feel-good clichés will be found in these pages. Rather it is counsel firmly rooted in the timeless truths of what it actually takes to have a lasting, real-life faith in our heavenly Father."

—REV. DR. DAVID R WELLS, MA, DD
GENERAL SUPERINTENDENT, PENTECOSTAL ASSEMBLIES OF CANADA

More than three million teens have heard the go-for-broke Christianity that Ron Luce preaches at Acquire the Fire events nationwide. In *Resilient* it is evident that this same message is for adults who desire to finish their race whatever may come.

—JIM GARLOW
SENIOR PASTOR, SKYLINE CHURCH, LA MESA, CALIFORNIA

In *Resilient*, Ron Luce encourages us to evaluate the tough questions of life and faith. Life on Planet Earth is not always easy. It can be confusing, chaotic, and contradictory. But through it all one thing remains the same: Jesus. He is our source of strength. As you read, you will find yourself encouraged, challenged, and equipped to be strong in God's grace no matter what unexpected twists life brings your way.

—JUDAH SMITH
LEAD PASTOR, THE CITY CHURCH, SEATTLE, WASHINGTON
NEW YORK TIMES BEST-SELLING AUTHOR OF *JESUS IS _____*.

Ron Luce is one of the most inspiring individuals I've ever met. His passion, energy, focus and drive are not only amazing but also uplifting. I'm honored to recommend Resilient as a firsthand testament of how living a life of faith is not a one-time decision but an ongoing determination to "pay the price" of following Jesus from beginning to end with our minds, hearts, strength, and wills.

—MARCOS WITT
FOUNDER CANZION PRODUCCIONES AND CANZION INSTITUTE
GRAMMY AWARD—WINNING PRODUCER, SINGER, AND PASTOR

Resilient is exactly what one has to be in order to survive life's many challenges. Ron Luce is the perfect one to share such a provocative story. Read the book, it could literally change your life!

—BISHIOP T. D. JAKES
NEW YORK TIMES BEST-SELLING AUTHOR

The faith that made America great withstood the most shocking of circumstances. In the spirit of our forefathers Ron Luce, through his book Resilient, inspires us to embrace the faith of great passion. If you want to finish strong and truly know your spiritual heritage in Christ, I would encourage you to let this book radically transform your life and perhaps the way you look at Christianity in the days that we live in of the 21st century church.

DAVID BARTON
PRESIDENT, WALL BUILDERS

His new book, *Resilient*, is consistent with Ron Luce's ongoing track record as a "real" church leader as well as a righteous one. He writes helpfully and pragmatically, delivering a work born in the wake of disaster and heartbreak—the point where others often become hopeless, give up, or become cynical and doubtful concerning God's purpose and plan for their lives.

I urge your reading. Ron's deserved reputation as the expert on "youth ministry" makes his writing pointed and palatable, but his life as a truly authentic, godly man introduces a depth which readers can grasp and a hope we all often need to be nourished.

—JACK W. HAYFORD
FOUNDER, THE KINGS UNIVERSITY, AND THE CHURCH ON THE WAY

I was given the great privilege of being invited into the lives of the Luce family and being a small part of their story. I went to serve them and offer some hope in their pain and instead found them serving me and bringing me hope in my pain.

—ERWIN RAPHAEL MCMANUS
FOUNDER, MOSAIC

Many of us can remember a phone call or message that made us stop in our tracks. Whether it was ten years ago or ten minutes ago, trouble is nothing new. God never said life would be easy. But how do we bounce back in our faith after something horrible has happened? In his book *Resilient* my friend Ron Luce shares his experiences as he struggled with unanswered questions and heartache after his daughter almost died in a plane crash. With a wealth of personal knowledge, practical guidelines, and spiritual wisdom on its pages, Ron's book will encourage you to build up your faith life to endure through the toughest adversity. However, this book is not just for those struggling through hard times; it's for anyone who wants to foster a resilient and enduring faith.

—ROBERT MORRIS
FOUNDING SENIOR PASTOR, GATEWAY CHURCH
BEST-SELLING AUTHOR, *THE BLESSED LIFE, FROM DREAM TO DESTINY*, AND
THE GOD I NEVER KNEW

RON LUCE

RESILIENT

CHARISMA
HOUSE

Cover design by Justin Evans

Visit the author's website at http://www.teenmania.com/.
Author's note: Videos related to the chapter topics can be found at http://resilientbook.com.

Library of Congress Cataloging-in-Publication Data:
Luce, Ron.
  Resilient / Ron Luce. -- First edition.
     pages cm
  ISBN 978-1-62136-971-4 (trade paper) -- ISBN 978-1-62136-972-1 (e-book)
  1. Christian life. 2. Resilience (Personality trait)--Religious aspects--Christianity. 3. Faith. 4. Trust in God--Christianity. I. Title.

BV4509.5.L78 2014
248.4--dc23

                              2014023791

First edition

14 15 16 17 18 — 9 8 7 6 5 4 3 2 1
Printed in the United States of America

CONTENTS

Part 4: The Fury of the Resilient

Becoming *Resilient* Study Guide

INTRODUCTION

At 4:30 p.m. on May 11, 2012, time seemed to stop. It happened when I got a phone call from a number I did not recognize. A woman was calling from the middle of Kansas. She began the conversation by asking, "Is this Ron Luce?"

I said, "Yes it is."

She said, "Your daughter Hannah is here with me and she is fine."

This is the phone call no parent wants to get. I continued with a question: "What do you mean Hannah is with you? She's on a plane. She's on her way to one of our events."

She repeated, "No, Hannah is with me. She's fine. She's been burned, but she's fine."

My mind raced in a million directions at once. How could she possibly know where my daughter was? After all, Hannah was in a small aircraft with four young men on their way to one of our Acquire the Fire conferences in Nebraska. Two of the young men were staff members and her good friends.

I continued probing for information. "What do you mean she's burned? Can I talk to her?"

The woman put Hannah on the phone. All my daughter could muster was, "Hi, Papa. I'm OK."

"What about the guys?" I asked. "Are they OK?"

The woman described the situation to me. "There's one young man…his name is Austin. He's been burned pretty badly. It looks like he made it to the road with Hannah, but I don't see anybody else."

I wondered, "How could this be possible? Hannah's supposed to be in a plane."

She continued, "I see smoke in the distance, it looks like the plane went down."

"Where are the other three guys?" I asked.

The caller continued very calmly. "I can't tell you anything about them. All I can tell you is that Hannah is here, and Austin is here."

I asked her to describe the scene some more. She said, "It looks like fire trucks are coming; ambulances are coming."

My world began spiraling out of control. After what seemed to be half an hour on the phone, I let the woman go and focused on making other contacts. First I called my wife Katie. I told her what was going on, and said we needed to get to the airport.

Even rushing to Dallas/Fort Worth International Airport meant taking a ninety-minute drive. The whole time one of us searched online for any updates on the plane wreck. Soon we saw news flashes about fatalities from a small plane crash in Kansas. When I learned where it was, I refused to believe the reports. "The Internet says all kinds of things that aren't true. Surely, this is one of those stories," I told myself.

To learn exactly what was happening on the ground, I made all kinds of phone calls. Finally,I reached the investigating officer on-site. I asked him, "What about the other three guys? Where are they?"

His answer rocked my world and my theology, all at once. He said, "Looks like those three were killed instantly when the plane crashed."

All of my disbelief came to a screeching halt. I couldn't argue with the on-site investigator. I remained speechless for quite some time, and I had a sickening feeling in the bottom of my gut.

We learned that Hannah was on her way to a burn unit in Kansas City, so we jumped on the first available flight. Meanwhile we sought updates on Austin's whereabouts and learned that he had been flown to Wichita, Kansas. Ninety percent of his body was burned, and he was on life support. People around the world prayed for him, and for Hannah as well.

At one o'clock in the morning, we reached Kansas City. Hannah was in ICU, on a respirator. Not only had thirty percent of her body received third-degree burns, but her lungs had also been burned. Doctors were not sure she was going to make it.

It is shocking to see your firstborn hooked up to what looks like a thousand tubes, wires, and monitors all keeping her alive. Katie and I were thrilled that she had survived; but we were also vexed beyond comprehension. How could three people (ultimately four, as Austin went to heaven the next day) have ended up beyond the bounds of the faith in which we were so confident? After all, they were young, and they loved God. They were at the top of their game and had graduated from college. They wanted to make a difference with their lives. They wanted to change the world.

For the next forty-eight hours we waited for Hannah to regain consciousness. It was one of the worst times in my life. Finally Hannah came out of her unconscious state. She was unable to speak, but she wrote notes here and there.

She kept asking, "How's Austin?"

Hannah knew Austin was alive when she last saw him. She knew from the beginning that the others had died, because she had to crawl over at least one friend's body to reach safety. She kept asking about Austin, and we kept distracting her with other things. Finally she wrote emphatically, in big letters: "WHAT ABOUT AUSTIN?"

Without the capacity even to vocalize words, I felt my eyes fill with tears. I just shook my head and grabbed her hand. With a breathing tube shoved down her throat and a million wires still attached to her body, Hannah cried profusely. I felt this was probably too much for her to deal with; I wanted to avoid the subject as long as possible. Hannah, however, would not be assuaged with anything but the facts.

Over the following week I attended four funerals of four men—Austin Anderson, Stephen Luth, Garrett Coble, and Luke Sheets—four days in a row. I did it at the insistence of Hannah and the invitation of the parents. Trying to explain the unexplainable to the parents and other mourners, I found myself reaching for words that seemed shallow. I tried my best to comfort them with thoughts I barely understood myself.

I made statements such as, "We don't understand why these things happen, but let's focus on what we do know: We do know that Jesus loves us. We do know that these men loved Jesus and are with Him right now. We do know that one day, He will comfort every heart and dry every tear, and we will be with Him forever."

Although I knew these were the facts, they seemed of little help to those suffering such intense grief.

QUESTIONING GOD

Over the next days, weeks, and months I found myself angry at God, but at the same time rejoicing. Have you ever been there—angry and happy at the same time? I was so thrilled that my daughter was alive. It seemed like it was a miracle that she survived the plane's plummet to Earth. The cockpit had filled with smoke. Luke, the pilot, had tried heroically to put the plane down even though he could not see past the windshield. How had Hannah survived the encroaching flames?

I only know that Hannah *did* survive. She managed to pull herself out of the plane moments before it exploded. Could it have been a miracle? Why weren't others saved if God was passing out miracles that day?

Yet while I was happy that my daughter was alive, I was angry at the circumstances. They did not line up with my theology. I prayed.

I had confidence in my prayers. For more than twenty years I had traveled all over the world and had big rigs, vans, trucks, and buses filled with staff and interns touring the country. Never had I experienced anything like this.

I told God that I did not like what happened. Whether He allowed it, caused it, or chose it as part of His strategic plan, I did not like it. As grateful as I was for my daughter's survival, I knew that other parents were dealing with unbearable grief. I told God, "I just don't understand."

What do we do as Christians when circumstances career out of control and we no longer understand what is going on? As followers of Christ, how do we react when the confidence we have in our faith is shaken? What happens when our theology and what we believe about God is called into question in a moment's time? How do we deal with situations that are so uncomfortable we can barely make sense of them? How can we possibly prepare ourselves for these moments? How do we develop the backbone of steel needed to take us through them?

All too often when these things happen, people slide off the road of their faith and back into the world's ways. They get mad at God and give up on Him. Their anger turns into resentment and even full-blown rebellion. What started as misunderstanding and deep hurt ends up becoming the reason they turn to atheism five, ten, or twenty years later: circumstances they could not explain.

A FAR BETTER OUTCOME

There is another possible outcome: *resilience*. It is the term we use when people bounce back from horrible experiences. Resilience is the grace to remain strong after going through something that almost breaks you.

How do we find that resilience? How can we prepare to be resilient before life's unexpected setbacks hit us in the face?

That is what this book is about. Together, we are about to explore the underpinnings of faith that lead us in one of two major directions: to give up or to be resilient.

You see, it is imperative *before* life hits us in the face that we build our foundation on the right belief system. Then, when things don't go according to our plans or theology, we will have a bedrock of trust in our heavenly Father.

As we embark on this journey through this book, my prayer is that we will be strengthened and prepared for whatever the enemy, the world, or life's circumstances might bring our way. Here's my other prayer: that the words of a well-known verse of Scripture will be for us, not just a nice bumper sticker, but the screaming anthem of our lives: "I *can* do all things through Christ who strengthens me" (Phil. 4:13, NKJV).

In other words, *I am resilient.*

PART 1: EXAMINE THE PREMISE OF OUR FAITH

W E MUST UNDERSTAND the culture surrounding us and the exact message we hear when we come to faith in Christ. Without the proper foundation, there is no chance of having a stable building. So many people falter in their faith, barely hanging on and eventually abandoning all they said they would die for. It happens because the foundation they had was not stable in the first place.

In Texas where we live, much of the ground is constantly shifting, which creates cracks in the walls and foundations of houses and other buildings. Many "pier companies" offer to drill deep below structures to install concrete and steel piers for foundations to rest upon. Unless this work is done, there is no possible way to have a home without cracks.

Many Christians' faith looks like the shifting ground I just described. We cannot possibly be resilient without establishing the proper foundation for our beliefs—both personally and culturally. So let's start by examining the foundation upon which much of Western Christianity has been built. Then we will build piers for our faith so that when the ground shifts our faith will not crack!

Chapter 1

FEEL-GOOD FAITH

T O TALK ABOUT building the kind of resilience that will allow us to bounce back (by the grace of God) no matter what hits us, we need to understand the cultural reality we face: we live in a *feel-good* world.

You could say that the American dream has its own soundtrack made of popular songs such as James Brown's "I Feel Good." For the most part in our culture we don't do the right thing; we do what we *feel like* doing. We don't do the wise thing; we do what we *feel like* doing. We don't even do what we committed to doing; we do what we *feel like* doing.

Imagine that you are in the mall, and you see a new outfit. You know you can't afford it, but you try it on anyway. You feel so good wearing it that you throw down the plastic and figure you'll find some way to pay for it. Maybe you stop by the dealership to test drive that car you have been eyeing. It feels so good driving down the road. You know your monthly budget won't stretch that far, but it feels so good that you decide that you will find a way.

Our culture is driven by feelings. People give their word in contracts all the time. Usually the majority of the text is about what happens if either party breaks their word. Contracts are written that way because people do what they feel like doing; they don't do what they committed to do. Couples stand before God and everybody else committing to stay together "till death us do part." They pledge their lives, their love, and their earthly wealth to each other for "as long as we both shall live." But a few years later they've lost that "loving feeling." They can't explain why, but now they have feelings for someone else.

The logic in our culture has become so convoluted that we believe we are not being true to ourselves if we stay with the person we chose to marry if we no longer have the goose bumps we felt when we first met. We say, "My feelings aren't there. I would be living a lie. I need to be with this other person who I now have feelings for."

It no longer matters what wreckage our decisions might cause. We try to deny how deeply the children's lives will be affected. Christians in leadership roles discount the pain felt by those observing the destruction of the marriage.

Somehow our culture has managed to convince us that our emotions are *the real us*. We are told that if we don't follow our feelings, we are not being authentic. If we do what is right instead of what we feel like doing, we are being phony. So in a world in which emotions were meant to *enhance our lives*, we have allowed them to *dominate our lives*. God gave us emotions so our lives would be richer and fuller. But we have allowed emotions to make us their slaves.

In a feel-good culture it is only natural that some people would surrender to *feel-good faith*. We make declarations to the Lord: "I'll do anything for You, Lord. I'll go to the ends of the earth for You. I'll even die for You." *Then we don't go to church when it rains because we might get our hair messed up.* We make vows to the Lord that we are quick to break the moment our feelings change.

Giving in to feelings of temptation and to sin are older than Christianity. But I am not talking about that here. I am talking about understanding the fundamental foundation of our belief system. In a culture that has taught us to do what we feel because "it can't be wrong if it feels so right," the biggest casualty is our Christianity. Because it is governed by feelings, it is a feel-good

Christianity—a faith in which we only follow the Lord, obey His commands, and read His Word when we feel like it.

It is no wonder that Christians find it so hard to have a strong backbone during hard times in America. If we are quick to break every other commitment when we feel like it, why would we treat our commitment to Christ any differently? Our cultural norms have settled into what we now deem to be "normal Christianity." We would never overtly say that we follow Him only when we feel like it; but for most part we Christians in America have succumbed to a faith that only engages when we are "*feelin' it.*"

It didn't feel good to bury four godly young men who had their whole lives ahead of them. I felt gut-wrenching anguish and did not understand the circumstances at all as I tried to comfort those families. As I appeared on *Today* with Matt Lauer and *Good Morning America* to describe how Hannah was doing (as it seemed the whole world was interested in her survival story), I had to choose to trust God. The circumstances violated my feelings and all natural inclinations. But understanding that *you are not your feelings* is the beginning of freedom from slavery to them. Just because you *feel* something does not mean you have to engage that emotion. If you follow every feeling, you will end up spiraling to the very bottom of the emotional pit where every emotional roller coaster ends up stopping, and you end up in a funk.

> In a world in which emotions were meant to *enhance our lives* we have allowed them to *dominate our lives.*

Christ didn't die so we could have feel-good faith. He died so our faith could be resilient.

BECOME RESILIENT

- Emotions are meant to enhance our lives not dominate our lves

- Emotions are not reality; they are momentary and they are temporary.

- If we allow our feelings to dominate our lives, we will end up enslaved by them.

Don't let feel-good faith leave you blindsided when life's unexpected challenges hit. Decide now that your faith will not be ruled by your feelings. Commit to follow the Lord no matter how you feel. That's the first step in building the kind of faith that is resilient.

Lord, I refuse to fall into the trap of feel-good faith. I will not abandon my commitment to You when situations in life get uncomfortable. I repent for all the times I have allowed my faith to be governed by my feelings. I choose to follow You no matter what, in Jesus's name. Amen.

Real-Life Resilient: Tamirat

"God have you forsaken me?" Tamirat was sharing a 13- × 13-foot cell with forty other inmates. The stench was incredible. Bodies were everywhere. Inmates had to take turns just to lie down. Yet Tamirat never felt so alone.[1]

Falsely accused by friends of offending the Muslim faith, Tamirat was arrested and tricked into signing a confession. Sentenced to three years in prison, he endured severe beatings from inmates and separation from his wife and children. Isolated and seemingly forgotten, Tamirat endured. Sixteen months into his prison term, charges against him were reduced. Released shortly afterward, Tamirat said, "May all glory be unto Him who has sustained and kept me through the dark hours. He has made me stronger and has built my faith."[2]

Chapter 2

GOD LOVES YOU AND HAS A WONDERFUL PLAN FOR YOUR LIFE?

O VER THE YEARS, some preachers have given people the impression that God is mad at Christians and all humanity. Other preachers have tried to counter the idea that God is angry by framing the messaging about our Christianity and our relationship with God in happier terms, saying such things as, "God loves you and has a wonderful plan for your life."

Dr. Bill Bright was one of the first champions of this phrase, setting people up from the get-go and informing them that God wanted only good for them. He was a mentor to me, and I was privileged to spend time with him in the last few days of his life. He would have never intended for the implications of this phrase to result in a feel-good commitment. In fact, I don't think I ever talked to him without being reminded that he "had been a slave of Christ for many years."

Of course, going to heaven *is* wonderful. Of course, having our sins forgiven is wonderful too. And, of course, living with the love of God overwhelming our souls is totally wonderful. However, to summarize the conversation by simply saying, "God loves you and has a wonderful plan for your life," has implications that in the long run cause many to grow weary in the faith.

If my chief motivation for coming to God is the implied promise that everything will be wonderful, then I will expect everything to be wonderful the moment I "pray that prayer." Of course, many pastors and preachers will add the caveat that praying the prayer doesn't mean all your problems will go away. However, there is an implication that from this point on things should be wonderful. "After all," we say, "I've given Him my heart, and He has a wonderful plan for my life. I *want* the wonderful plan."

If we were to define the word *wonderful* in its most literal sense, we would say it means "full of wonder." So in His wonderful plan, for example, we will be awestruck by His presence, stunned by how He wants to use us, in awe of how He delivers us, and shocked by how He continually provides for us. In that case *wonderful* might be the appropriate word to use.

The connotation hints that everything will be pleasant and fun, and we will tiptoe through tulips for the rest of our lives. We know that we still live in a world full of sin, struggle, and challenges. But the good news is, because we have committed our lives to the Lord, we don't ever have to face these things alone.

The problem is, if we come to faith and follow Christ believing that everything will be wonderful, as soon as something that's not wonderful comes our way, we will quietly reason, "That's not in my contract. That's not what I signed up for. I signed up for the wonderful plan. I signed up to tiptoe through the tulips and have love and ooey-gooey feelings for the rest of my life."

If we really and truly understand that Jesus asked us to take up our cross and follow Him, and if we face up to His statement about enduring to the end and being saved (Matt. 16:24; 24:13), we cannot miss the implication that there will be something to endure. Challenges *will* come, as we will discuss more in later chapters.

Consider the earliest followers of Christ. Almost all of His disciples were martyred in some way for their faith. They also suffered in life. Look at Paul and Silas, who were jailed and whipped again and again. Paul described the challenges they faced:

> We put no stumbling block in anyone's path, so that our ministry will not be discredited. Rather, as servants of God we commend ourselves in every way: in great endurance; in troubles, hardships and distresses; in beatings, imprisonments and riots; in hard work, sleepless nights and hunger; in purity, understanding, patience and kindness; in the Holy Spirit and in sincere love; in truthful speech and in the power of God; with weapons of righteousness in the right hand and in the left; through glory and dishonor, bad report and good report; genuine, yet regarded as impostors; known, yet regarded as unknown; dying, and yet we live on; beaten, and yet not killed; sorrowful, yet always rejoicing; poor, yet making many rich; having nothing, and yet possessing everything.
>
> —2 Corinthians 6:3–10

Paul endured all these hardships for the sake of the gospel. It would be hard to hear his testimony and say, "He signed up for the wonderful life plan."

Even in our day it might be more appropriate to say that God loves us and has an *adventurous* plan for our lives or a *dangerous* plan for our lives or a *fantastic* and *unpredictable* plan for our lives. But wonderful? Not so much.

As I sat with Hannah in the ICU, knowing that four young men had died and their families were facing unimaginable grief, I didn't feel wonderful. Those first few days after the plane crash were a blur of shock, sadness, and concern. The news of the tragedy was all over the news, and we were receiving a flood of questions about Hannah's condition and, thankfully, much-needed prayers. Our whole Teen Mania team was mourning the loss of four young lives. No one expected God's plan to include anything like this. It was a miracle that Hannah was alive, but she would still need skin grafts for the third-degree burns she sustained on the back of her hands and her lower left leg. Our hearts were heavy. *Wonderful* is the last word I would use to describe how we felt.

When challenges hit us (and hit us they will), or when things that are less-than wonderful come our way, what will we do? If our expectation is completely and totally based on the idea that everything will be great once we pray a certain prayer, that same expectation will shape our entire perspectives of what it means to be a follower of Christ—and we will be sorely disappointed, as many people are.

Many people who "prayed that prayer" (we will talk about what that prayer is in the next chapter) have since found out that not everything about following Christ is rosy. Because of what they believed at the beginning, they now feel they were lied to by the preacher or by God. They end up saying, "How can I follow a preacher or a God who lies to me? How can I trust anyone who promises me a wonderful life but doesn't give me one?"

Here is the point: *the way in which we understand the gospel when we first come to Christ dictates how we will live from that point forward.* Our understanding of what we are committing to and what we are receiving when we decide to follow Christ is of the highest importance.

> If our expectation is completely and totally based on the idea that everything will be great once we pray a certain prayer, that same expectation will shape what it means to be a follower of Christ—and we will be sorely disappointed.

Could it be that the current landslide of people in America turning away from the church and their faith is a result of a faulty foundation? Could it be that our interpretation of the gospel is so shrouded by the "feel-good" culture that our embracing of faith in Christ comes with all kinds of "reasonable" ways to back out if things don't feel good anymore?

If we are to be resilient lifelong followers of Christ, something has to change. Many Christians and preachers have been over promising and under-delivering. We promise people that everything is going to be wonderful and either fail to define what that means or expect people to define it on their own. As a result we end up with spiritual carnage—pseudo followers of Christ who become disillusioned in their faith. They become negative advertising for Christianity, the ones who say, "Yeah, I tried that Christianity thing, and it didn't work."

As living examples of a seemingly failed experiment called *Christianity*, the disillusioned become our worst enemies.

BECOME RESILIENT

- Yes, God loves you and has a wonderful plan for your life, but that doesn't mean life will be easy.

- Jesus called us to take up our cross and follow Him. That implies that challenges *will* come.

- When those trials hit, we are not alone. God is with us. But the Christian life is not about avoiding pain; it is about following Christ no matter what.

Lord, guard my heart from becoming disillusioned when challenges come my way. Forgive me for those times when I thought my life in Christ was supposed to be easy. I choose to follow You, not so my life will be wonderful, but because You are the only one who deserves my devotion. Because You died I have life, and I give my life back to You. Whatever comes my way, good or bad, I trust You. I will not back down from standing in faith, in Jesus's name. Amen.

Chapter 3

PASSIVE FAITH

I CAN'T TELL YOU how frustrated I was after I finally got turned on to Jesus at sixteen. I had been raised in church—several dead, dry, boring, and pathetic churches. Even though I sensed God speaking to me and wooing me at times, not once did my faith ever come alive during those first sixteen years.

At the age of twelve I went forward to the altar because I felt the Lord wanted me to do so. No one else went forward that day, just me. I didn't know what going forward meant or what I should do while I was up there. As the choir sang the closing hymn, the pastor leaned over to me, waiting for me to say something. But I had no idea know what to say.

Finally I said, "I felt like the Lord wanted me to come up here. He's been speaking to me for two weeks."

The pastor replied, "Praise the Lord, brother! Why don't you go talk to this lady right here?"

As I sat down on the front pew, the lady began filling out a card. "What's your name?" she asked. "What's your address? Would you like to be baptized?"

All of a sudden I thought, "So, *that's* how people get baptized! They come up and fill out a card."

When the service was over, the pastor brought me in front of the church and read the card aloud. He told everyone my name and asked those who were in favor of receiving me as a member of the church to say, "Aye."

Apparently enough people said, "Aye."

Then the pastor said, "Come up and greet him."

People lined up at the front of the church to greet me. Many were crying and most of them hugged me. I remember thinking, "Why are they crying? What happened? What are they sad about?" I honestly didn't know *what* had happened.

Finally, sometime after church that day, my mom said, "So you became a Christian today."

I thought, "Really? Is that what I did?"

No one told me anything when I went forward. If someone had made clear what I was doing at the front of the church—if someone had explained that my decision was a fork in the road of my life—I might have been spared a lot of pain and confusion through my teenage years. But no one told me anything.

WHERE PASSIVITY BEGINS

Coming to Christ is a big deal, and *how* we come to Christ is just as big a deal. In this chapter we are going to look at several common ways in which the gospel is presented so we can identify some significant fallacies affecting the body of Christ.

In the Western world over the past fifty years many gospel presentations have produced a passive mental assent to the faith. The approaches I'm going to describe in this chapter seems like *normal* Christianity because we have heard them preached so much. But as we will soon see they don't lead people to a strong foundation for their faith. The messaging that draws us to Christ is vitally important because *the framework and understanding we have when we first come to faith informs the way we live our faith and determines how faith affects our lives.*

If we have to beg people to come to Christ, then we will have to beg them to read their Bibles, beg them to attend church, beg them to live holy and keep on loving God. Something is missing in our presentation of the gospel when we have to prop people up and beg them to stay engaged. We will consider common salvation messaging and the implications of each. The truth is that most of them have been passive, resulting in Christians who are passive in their faith. The danger is apparent: passive Christianity cannot produce resilient Christians.

Let's take a good look at some familiar approaches to presenting the gospel so we can see where we might be missing it.

"Would You Accept Christ?"

The first time I brought up this subject to Dr. Jack Hayford, he seemed startled. Dr. Hayford, who has spent decades hearing and preaching the gospel, had become both a mentor and a member of our board of directors for Teen Mania. At lunch I asked him, "So what's the deal about accepting Christ? Why is that preached so much? I don't see the idea of accepting Christ anywhere in the Bible."

> The framework and understanding we have when we first come to faith informs the way we live our faith and determines how faith affects our lives.

Dr. Hayford spun around and looked at me with a laser focus. He said, "That's a very good point. Let's talk about it."

We talked about hearing even the most famous preachers ask, "Would you like to accept Christ?" Yet it just so happens that Jesus never asked anyone to accept Him. None of the apostles ever asked anyone to accept Him, either. In fact, the words are a strange concoction. Accepting something is a passive act. You are not going after it; you are merely allowing it into your life.

Think about it: we would never ask, "Will you accept Joe as a friend?" But for some reason, we think it is OK to ask people to accept Christ as their Lord and Savior. Acceptance is a familiar concept in our culture. Every day we hear, "We accept Visa," or, "We accept Master Card." So it seems OK to us to accept Christ.

The implication is that because you're accepting Him, you're giving Him a good deal. "Yes," we say, "I'll accept You, Lord." It's almost as if Jesus is living under a bridge, out in the cold and needing a place to stay. He doesn't know where to go, so we ask, "Would you accept Him? Would you give Him a place to stay?" We act as if He needs a friend, and we are giving Him a break. Actually, when Jesus comes into our lives, *He's the one giving us a break* by forgiving us and breathing life into our dead hearts. He is the one accepting us!

What is meant by the term "accepting Christ" is clear if you are a theologian. It means that if you accept His sacrifice on the cross as propitiation for your sins, you are accepting the reality that He paid the price so you don't have to. You are accepting by faith the fact that He died in your place. That is all great, but the phrase "accepting Christ" doesn't communicate this very well, especially to someone who has never gone to church. Most people who know nothing of God would not understand the theological underpinnings of accepting Christ.

The issue reminds me of the commonly used expression *Howdy*. Until recently I had no idea that the question "How do you do?" had been reduced to "Howdy." That is what we have done with the idea of accepting Christ. It is a kind of shorthand for a larger concept.

When we invite people to accept Him, they respond by raising their hands, going forward, and praying a prayer. But in all reality what do they really commit to? They have no idea where the terminology began or what the speaker might actually mean when he asks them to "accept Christ." They only know that they feel moved and want to get closer to God. They take the step, but they cannot wrap their minds around it. Yes, Jesus has come to live inside them. In the best possible case He has transformed their lives. Yet they have a passive approach to their relationships with Him because they merely *accepted* Him, whatever that means.

"Would You Like a *Personal Relationship* With Christ?"

If you have been in church for any length of time at all, you have heard this question asked often: "Would you like to have a personal relationship with Christ?" You might even have asked someone the question yourself.

The problem is the terminology. It is a strange way of describing a relationship with someone. Now we know that when Jesus comes to live inside us, it *is* very personal. It is the most personal relationship of all. He already knows all of our thoughts and intentions and everything in our hearts. However, if you or I were to introduce a good friend to someone would we say, "Hi. This is Johnny. He is a friend with whom I have a personal relationship"?

Why would we need to say it? If Johnny is a friend, the relationship is implied. It should be obvious that the relationship is personal.

In our modern Christianity we ask, "Would you like a personal relationship with Christ?" Then someone answers, "Yes." He or she comes forward, prays a prayer, and claims a personal relationship with Christ. But is it really personal? Is it a very deep relationship?

Not necessarily. When you have a deep, close, personal relationship with someone, you don't have to say so. It is obvious to everyone. I don't have to tell people that I have a deep personal relationship with my wife, Katie. I don't even use those words. The fact that we have a personal relationship is apparent because of how we carry ourselves. People see our marriage and realize that our relationship is deep.

For too many people God seems far off and aloof. Saying He is almighty and all-powerful does not fully describe His nature. It is important for us to realize that He is a person who wants to share deep, personal closeness with us as human beings. Just think about it: why do we, in a human family, cherish those we love, cry when we lose them, and weep when we are reunited after a long time apart? How could an aloof being create a species that is so engaged in personal relationships on so many levels? A personal God made humans in His image to appreciate personal, loving relationships. He made us to walk with Him in the cool of the day as Adam did (see Gen. 3:8).

We were made for the most personal of all relationships: a relationship with our Creator. What I fear is the possibility that we have substituted a deep, authentic relationship with Christ for the words personal relationship. *Talking* about having a personal relationship is not necessarily the same as actually having one. The relationship should scream that it's personal without our having to say a word.

It is almost as though we invite people into this personal relationship with Christ because the words sound spiritual and produce good feelings. Because the words *sound* spiritual, we don't want to ask what they mean. We don't want to sound unspiritual or uninformed. Instead we go along as though we understand our "Christianese." We smile politely, yet very few actually live out the authentic expression of the words *personal relationship*.

"Do You Want That Love, That Joy, That Peace...?"

Too often we hear only the upside of coming to Christ. We are told, "If you're not full of love, if you're not full of joy or peace, if you're empty on the inside, come. He will fill you up!"

That is all true. He *will* fill us up. Yet, I'm afraid, the choice of words can easily build another faulty foundation upon which too many people build their Christianity. Of course, with Christ at the center of our lives, we are overwhelmed with love, because He *is* love. He is also the prince of peace so He floods our hearts with peace.

The challenge with presenting the gospel this way is that we end up coming to Christ to get something and not to give ourselves to Him. We come with conditions: "As long as I get this, then I'll come. As long as I can keep this, then I'll stay." In other words, we come to get the joy, the love, and the peace. But the moment we don't feel joy or peace, our faith gets shaky.

If getting stuff is the crux upon which our whole relationship with Christ is measured, we'll find it hard to keep our commitment to Him when times get tough.

What if we had a completely different paradigm? What if we understood that *God is the rightful owner of this universe and the rightful owner of our lives*? How would our faith be affected if we understood that when He breathed into us, He gave us life itself.

When I gave my life back to Him, He deserved it because He was the One who gave me life in the first place. Instead of coming to Him because we want this joy or love or whatever we hope to get out of the deal, what if we came because we recognized that He is the God of the universe? What if our perspective was more like A. W. Tozer's. He said:

> God being Who and What He is, and we being who and what we are, the only thinkable relation between us is one of full lordship on His part and complete submission on ours. We owe Him every honor that it is in our power to give Him.[1]

The fact is, when we give our lives back to Him, we are simply giving Him what He deserves. He doesn't owe us peace or joy or fulfillment. We owe Him everything.

"If You Died Right Now, Do You Know Where You Would Go?"

This motivation to follow Christ is easily one of the most common. We motivate people to "pray that prayer" knowing they don't want to go to hell forever. Somewhere along the line we in the Western world boiled down the idea of following Christ to a means of avoiding of hell. The threat is: if you *don't* pray the prayer, then you *will* go to hell.

The truth is that Jesus talked very little about going to hell. I am, of course, grateful that our Savior rescues us from an eternity without God—without a doubt! However, when the fear of hell is what motivates us to come to Christ, it poses potential challenges to our faith. Remember: the premise under which we come to Christ shapes *how* we live out our Christianity. So the question is this: *When people come to Christ, are they running from hell or running to Jesus?*

If we urge people to run from hell, then they will be motivated by fear and judgment. To avoid hell they're inclined to think of all the bad things they shouldn't do so they don't end up in hell. This could easily turn into a do-good list. They think, "As long as I do all these things, I won't end up in hell. But if I mess up, I'll just pray a quick prayer to Jesus to forgive me."

However, if we were to present Jesus, even a glimpse of Him, in all His beauty and splendor and let people's hearts be captured by the wonder of Christ, that would be a different story. Instead of following Jesus so they can get out of hell, people would fall in love with who He is and follow Him because He is their life's passion. They would pursue Him with every ounce of energy they possessed because they've been swept off their feet. And He would take them on an amazing journey for the rest of their lives.

Please note that Jesus never motivated people by saying, "If you don't follow Me, you will go to hell." He said things such as, "I am the way, the truth, and the life. No one comes to the Father except through Me" (John 14:6, NKJV). He didn't use the word *hell* there. He said, "If you want the hookup between you and the Father God who made the universe, I'm the only way to get it."

Jesus constantly provoked people's curiosity about the kingdom of God. He made them imagine what it would be like to connect with the King of the universe and to have His rule over their lives. We would do well to do the same.

"ALL YOU HAVE TO DO IS..."

Of all the approaches I have heard, this one riles me the most. I understand that when people use this phrase, they're not intentionally softselling the gospel. Yet for all practical purposes they are. What they mean to say is: "You don't have to do rules. You don't have to do regulations. You don't have to whip yourself the way some religions require, or beat yourself in order to please God." They are trying to say, "He's paid the price for you. Therefore, you don't have to pay it."

Even so, it becomes a soft sell of the gospel. Jesus says things such as, "Take up [your] cross, and follow Me" (Matt. 16:24). He means that we should prepare to die when we follow Him. He points out that we are going in one direction, but He wants us to stop, turn around, and go completely in the other direction. He sees us going down paths that lead to destruction—paths of selfishness, me-centerdness, "coolness," the culture, and cliques. He says, "I want you to stop and do a 180 and head in the other direction."

That is *all you have to do*: give complete control of your life to Jesus's lordship.

During His earthly ministry Jesus gave people the choice. If they were not ready to give up everything and let Him have complete control, He was fine with that. In fact, when people were eager to say, "I'll follow You, Lord!" He would urge them to think it over. He asked, "Are you sure? Have you counted the cost?"

> Suppose one of you wants to build a tower. Won't you first sit down and estimate the cost to see if you have enough money to complete it? For if you lay the foundation and are not able to finish it, everyone who sees it will ridicule you, saying, "This person began to build and wasn't able to finish." Or suppose a king is about to go to war against another king. Won't he first sit down and consider whether he is able with ten thousand men to oppose the one coming against him with twenty thousand? If he is not able, he will send a delegation while the other is still a long way off and will ask for terms of peace. In the same way, those of you who do not give up everything you have cannot be my disciples.
>
> —Luke 14:28–33

"Are you sure?" Jesus asked. He constantly tapped the brakes of people's zeal. Instead of wooing or begging them to follow Him, He invited them to reconsider.

We do the opposite. We soft sell the gospel, saying, "All you have to do is come forward, pray this prayer, and lift your hand." Then, when they come to church the next week, the preacher says, "Being a Christian is about more than praying a prayer. You've got to read your Bible and live holy."

Christians hear that and in the back of their minds say, "Wait a minute. I thought you said last week that all I have to do is come forward, pray a prayer, and lift my hand. I didn't sign up for the version where I'd have to read my Bible and share my faith and live holy. I bought into the 'all you have to do' version of the gospel— the 'I'm going to barely slide under the pearly gates' version of Christianity."

And so we end up thinking there are two kinds of Christians: the real radical ones who read their Bibles, live holy, don't sleep around, and don't get drunk, and the "all you have to do" types who pray the quick prayer, earn their get-out-of-hell-free card, live any way they want, and think of the Bible as a list of good suggestions.

I don't see this in Scripture. There are not two kinds of Christians; there is only one kind. No one is going to sneak under the pearly gates. Everyone who goes in will do it with the gates wide open.

"JUST PRAY THIS PRAYER WITH ME..."

When I finally got on fire for the Lord when I was sixteen years old, I wanted to tell my friends about Jesus. I searched and searched my Bible for that prayer—the sinner's prayer that gets people saved. It seemed like a neat little formula, the certain "magical" words you have people say and then—abracadabra!—they go to heaven.

After all my searching and searching, someone finally told me that the prayer is not in the Bible. I remember thinking, "How can the sinner's prayer—the most important prayer of all—not be in the Bible? And if it's not in the Bible, how am I going to know the formula to get people into heaven?"

Here is the problem: we have reduced our holy faith from the almighty God into man-made formulas. We get mad when we can't find the right one. We get frustrated when we realize that our formulas do not work. It is much easier to perform a ritual than to have a heart revolution that transforms the way people live. Saying "just pray this prayer with me" is so much easier than inviting people to surrender their all to Christ.

Don't get me wrong; as I hold events all across the country attended by thousands of teenagers every week, I lead them in a prayer. But I am very careful to say, "Listen, I'm just helping you with the words. This prayer needs to come from your heart, from the bottom of your soul. It's a connection with God. It's the beginning of a relationship. It's like the first time you're talking to somebody who's real about something authentic in your heart. It's not the end of the conversation; it's the beginning."

"Just pray this prayer with me" sounds like some kind of secret handshake. The suggestion is, if you learn the secret handshake, you will get into heaven. What's that about? I remember speaking at a big event organized by another ministry. It was an amazing time. Many students came forward. They prayed. They connected with God. They repented. Tears flowed all over the place.

When I was finished, the leader of the event said, "Now those of you who came up here, I want you to repeat this prayer with me."

Those teens had already poured their guts out to God and totally wrapped their whole lives around Christ. But in this man's mind they were not saved yet. They didn't have a real encounter with Christ because they didn't say the exact "sinner's prayer" his denomination espoused.

The exact words are not the issue. Paul explained the bigger picture in his letter to the Romans:

> "The word is near you; it is in your mouth and in your heart," that is, the message concerning faith that we proclaim: If you declare with your mouth, "Jesus is Lord," and believe in your heart that God raised him from the dead, you will be saved. For it is with your heart that you believe and are justified, and it is with your mouth that you profess your faith and are saved.
> —ROMANS 10:8–10

We'll talk more later about what these verses mean. Suffice to say here that many preachers believe that if you don't say certain exact words, then you're not saved. Ironically they believe that as long as you say the "right" words, you are saved. Whether you mean them, believe them, or understand them is not the point.

This is like "abracadabra" Christianity. Because of it we end up with people who have said the words and done the formulas. They justify doing whatever they want because they have the secret hand-shake down.

"HAVE YOU *RECEIVED* THE LORD?"

We hear this wording a lot, and of all the passive approaches we have discussed, this one is actually in the Bible (once):

> Yet to all who did receive him, to those who believed in his name, he gave the right to become children of God—children born not of natural descent, nor of human decision or a husband's will, but born of God.
>
> —JOHN 1:12–13

The problem is that the way we understand the word *received* is very passive. It's like when you receive a gift: you stand there and someone else does the giving. However, the Greek word in John's Gospel is not passive. The word translated "received" is *lambano*. It essentially means to grab hold of something and never let go.[2]

It may be better said that those who take hold of Jesus and never let go get the power to become sons and daughters of God. The difference is huge: one understanding produces passive faith; the other produces aggressive faith. In one case we stand back and receive; in the other we take hold and embrace.

Too many of the words we use are passive. Maybe the intention is to be sure that people are not working for their salvation. To that I give a hearty amen. But the phrase has also lulled the Western church to sleep. A sleeping church is not a resilient church; it will not hold up under fire.

"WILL YOU TRUST THE LORD THIS MORNING?"

You have probably heard it from the pulpit: "Will you trust the Lord this morning?" This is another passive phrase. Trusting the Lord with your whole life is not passive at all, provided you see yourself as being completely, totally, and utterly dependent on Him for your salvation, your life, and even your breath. However, we're trusting Him to forgive us. The better question may be: Do we trust Him enough to take Him at His Word? Do we trust Him so much that we follow what He says, even when we don't understand it? Do we trust Him when nothing in our lives seems to make sense? Do we trust Him enough to trust His opinion from His Word over our own opinions and feelings?

Trust explained like that makes a lot more sense because it is more active than passive—an active dependency rather than a shallow mental assent. Please understand that I am not pointing fingers at any one preacher or stream of Christianity. I am saying that the Christian faith is in crisis in America and in all of Western culture. We have people who go to church every Sunday yet most data shows they don't live much differently from the rest of the world. Every preacher and every follower of Christ must examine the foundation of our belief system and the kind of results it produces in our lives and in the lives of those we would woo to follow Christ.

To be resilient we *must* build our faith on the proper foundation in order to withstand the earthquakes that will surely come.

BECOME RESILIENT

- *How* we come to Christ matters because the understanding we have when we first come to faith informs the way we live our faith and how faith affects our lives.

- Coming to faith in Christ was never meant to be a passive mental assent. God wants us to do more than accept Him—He wants us to follow Him, to pursue Him, to grab hold of Him, and never let go.

- When you're in a relationship that's personal, it shows. We shouldn't have to *say* we're in a personal relationship with Christ. The reality that our relationship is personal should scream from our lives.

- Our faith cannot be conditional. We don't give our lives to Christ so we will receive love, peace, or joy. We give Him our lives because He deserves it. *He is the rightful owner of the universe and the rightful owner of our lives.* He deserves *everything.*

- The sinner's prayer is not a magical formula. Rather than reciting a special prayer, God would much rather we have a heart revolution that transforms the way we live.

God wants us to trust Him but not in a passive way. He wants us to trust His Word and His character, even when we don't understand what's going on. He wants us to trust His opinion over our own opinion and feelings. He wants us to actively depend on Him. If you want to commit to truly following Christ, take a minute to give Him complete control.

Lord, forgive me if I have allowed my faith to become little more than a passive mental assent. I choose to grab hold of You and never let go. You gave me my life, and I give it back to You because You deserve it. May my heart be captured more and more each day by who You are. I give You complete control. I've counted the cost, and I choose to follow You. I abandon my life for Yours. May my life produce good fruit that woos others to follow You, in Jesus's name. Amen.

Chapter 4

THE "THEOLOGY OF COMPLACENCY"

You have seen how these passive ways of presenting the gospel have produced in us something completely opposite of what Jesus intended. They have also made it appear that anyone who is passionate about living holy or changing the world either has a "holier than thou" attitude or is a works-oriented Christian.

For many people the idea of living holy and really doing their best to live like Jesus is just one option for a Christian. They say, "I'm not really religious. I'm not really into rules. I believe Jesus loves me just as I am." Some even say, "Oh, you're into all those rules and holiness. You're just trying to earn favor with God. I don't think we can do anything to earn His love, and so I'm not into that."

When they hear that you are taking up your cross and following Jesus, they accuse you of trying to work for your salvation. Too many "regular" Christians will mock your passion for Christ and justify their fleshly pleasures by saying, "God wants me to be happy."

Whether their idea of being happy involves drinking, dancing, or other activities, they find a way to excuse it. Complacency has dulled their spiritual senses and caused them to misunderstand the faith. Instead of seeing Christ as master, *He has become for them a kind of life-enhancement drug.*

Before we move on, let me be clear: the Bible does not condemn all drinking. However, much of what Christians do in the name of social drinking is a far cry from the joy-filled life in Christ that diminishes the desire for sensual pleasures.

Honestly I never need a drink to "take the edge off." I cast my cares on Him. The kind of living that looks to alcohol to "take the edge off" only drowns out a passionate response to the things of Christ. It has produced a "theology of complacency" that strips away any sense of destiny. It makes you forget that you are here for a reason. The idea of making your mark on the world is mocked. You might even be accused of being overly ambitious. This theology actually tries to find spiritual ways to justify compromise and half-hearted following of Christ.

Jesus did not come to be our therapist! He did not come to just enhance our lives and make them a "little bit better"! He did not give His life to be an add-on to our lives as if He was something we buy from a late-night infomercial! He came to totally revolutionize our lives!

When you are accused of being too ambitious for Christ, realize that the accusations are less about you and more about other people's complacency. Those who are stuck in it tend to justify going nowhere and feeling godly about it. They take pride in the fact that they are not "striving in their faith." Yet the fact is that *no one ever made a mark on the world for God with this kind of complacency.*

FINDING THE TREASURE

The remedy for the "theology of complacency" is simple: fall in love with Jesus. When you fall in love with Jesus, you make a discovery. The discovery is so big, you willingly change your whole life for it. Scripture explains: "The kingdom of heaven is like treasure hidden in a field. When a man found it, he hid it again, and then in his joy went and sold all he had and bought that field" (Matt. 13:44).

This is the treasure we have found. It is not by human effort; it is because He drew us by His grace. But we made the discovery. It captured our imagination and our hearts so that we want more of Him and His Spirit. We are mesmerized, smitten by what we have heard. The discovery sweeps us off our feet. Jesus's love is so great and His sacrifice so fantastic that we simply cannot keep it to ourselves.

> He did not come to just enhance our lives and make them a "little bit better!"... He came to totally revolutionize our lives.

Many people have not made this discovery. They know there is something good about God, but they follow Him out of obligation. They know there is some kind of treasure because everybody talks about it. They feel they ought to get it somehow, or logically convince other people to do so. But without the treasure in their hearts, they do not feel obligated to tell anyone to do anything great.

People have asked me many times: "How have you stayed so passionate all these years?"

My only response is: "I don't try to be passionate. But I know there are things of the flesh that need to die. When I take them to the cross, they die, and that death produces life."

It is amazing: when part of me dies, it makes more room for the life of God to fill me up!

There is more of God available than we ever dreamed possible. The Spirit-filled life we desire provokes us to seek the deep things of God. We long for the discovery of the treasure in deepening ways. This passion for more of Him is all-consuming. If you really want that passion you have to take your flesh to the cross.

LEAVE COMPLACENCY BEHIND

If you feel stuck in complacency, you don't have to stay there. When you discover that the Creator of the universe sent His Son *for you*, your complacency will be replaced with a passion for Him.

Isaiah recognized the treasure and saw the Creator in all His glory. Just read these words:

> Say to the towns of Judah, "Here is your God!" See, the Sovereign LORD comes with power, and he rules with a mighty arm. See, his reward is with him, and his recompense accompanies him. He tends his flock like a shepherd: he gathers the lambs in his arms and carries them close to his heart; he gently leads those that have young. Who has measured the waters in the hollow of his hand, or with the breadth of his hand marked off the heavens? Who has held the dust of the earth in a basket, or weighed the mountains on the scales and the hills in a balance? Who can fathom the Spirit of the LORD, or instruct the LORD as his counselor? Whom did the LORD consult to enlighten him, and who taught him the right way? Who was it that taught him knowledge, or showed him the path of understanding? Surely the nations are like a drop in a bucket; they are regarded as dust on the scales; he weighs the islands as though they were fine dust. Lebanon is not sufficient for altar fires, nor its animals enough for burnt offerings. Before him all the nations are as nothing; they are regarded by him as worthless and less than nothing.
>
> —ISAIAH 40:9–17

Do you realize who this God is? He is the God of the universe who made everything that is good—*and He loves you.* When His Son came into the world, He was not wrapped in fancy linen. He came humbly, in a manger. The world never expected God to be humble, yet He humbled Himself for our sakes.

The angels knew what happened and could not contain themselves. They broke through the bounds of heaven shouting, "Glory, hallelujah!" The angels were so big and so massive that they had to calm the shepherds who saw them, saying, "Don not be afraid" (Luke 2:10).

The event was profound, because God's plan was. This was God sending His Son to invade the human scene and bring us life. This was Emmanuel, *God with us.* Imagine—we serve a God who wants to be with us!

Have you made this discovery? The man who found the treasure in Matthew 13:44 did. He was so excited about the discovery he got rid of everything else. His response had nothing to do with obligation. No one had to tell him to sell all of his stuff so he could get the field. No one made him feel obligated. He didn't dread selling all he had. He realized that what he had was nothing compared to the treasure he found in the field.

This is the response God's looking for from us. When we discover Him, He doesn't want us to act out of obligation and think, "Oh, I can't have any fun. I'm walking away from the world." He wants to hear us say, "I found something that's better than the cure for cancer. I've found the answer to all of my dreams."

About two weeks after the plane crash I was sitting with Hannah in the hospital after she had endured a five-and-a-half-hour skin graft. As I sat there watching all the beeping screens and flashing numbers on the monitors and machines connected to her body, I couldn't help but think about all the time and money that went into creating each of those pieces of technology. I wondered how many people over how many years spent their lives doing research then refining that research to develop each device. I wondered how much money and time went into creating the technology that was working to restore Hannah's health.

Then I thought about all the medical professionals and nurses and all the years they spent training for their professions and learning how to operate each of those pieces of technology. Then I thought about the people in the room next door to Hannah and how the same ingenuity and investment was working to restore their health and the health of every patient on every floor of the entire hospital. Then I thought about the thousands of hospitals and the millions of medical professionals across the United States and around the world—all working with the hope to save and restore lives.

It seems like a massive investment—and it is—but the investment was made because we, as the human race, value life so much. People from different religions and different walks of life value saving lives so much that they think it's worth investing in the medical industry, whether with their time or their resources.

Then I thought about the recipients of all of that technology and medical expertise, and I wondered if they really understood the value of the investment that had been made. Sure, the hospital bills will come due, but do those patients truly understand all the years of study and research and financing being poured into them the moment they need it most? When they are restored and out of the hospital, do they live in such a way that shows they know how much they were valued?

In other words, do they value their own life enough to live to make it meaningful? Or do they just think to themselves, "I sure am glad I have been given a few more years to live," but then sit in front of the TV or a computer screen for the rest of their lives?

As I sat there with Hannah, I thought, "What a vast juxtaposition." People who don't even know these patients value them so much that they would devote themselves to saving the lives of strangers. And yet so many people live without purpose and without making any kind of contribution to the world. Even though their lives have been valued by others, they don't value it themselves. They merely exist.

As Christians we can see the metaphor clearly. God so valued us that He made a huge investment in us to save and restore our lives. Do we reciprocate? Do we value what He's done in us to the point that we refuse to live a purposeless life? So we refuse to take that investment He's made in us for granted?

I'm inspired to live a life that is more worthy of the sacrifice and the value that was placed on me. We could never deserve the sacrifice Jesus made for us. But at least we could attempt to live in a way that demonstrates our deep appreciation of the value God places on us. Our response should be to refuse to take this life for granted, but instead to live a life that makes a difference because we understand we were saved for a reason.

If you dread trading in your flesh to gain the kingdom, instead of merely going through the motions, go back and rediscover the treasure. Make sure that what you found is what God intended for you. Make sure you discovered the true treasure and not just something you thought you might need someday.

This is not about legalism and following the rules; it is about getting closer to God and letting His love invade us. I am not talking about becoming a cookie-cutter Christian who carefully follows the dos and don'ts. I am talking about being a person whose soul has been filled with God's joy. As the Scripture says, "The joy of the Lord is your strength" (Neh. 8:10). Only He can make us resilient. He does not ask us to buckle down and try to be strong; *He makes us strong.*

When you find the treasure and recognize its value, your heart cannot help but change. You become desperate for more of God, earnest in desiring Him, and passionate in your response to Him. You feel a torrent of love for Him—you are completely smitten. If you have languished in the theology of complacency, it is time to allow your heart to change—not by stifling yourself, but by receiving His preemptive grace, the grace that allows you to discover the treasure in the first place.

To leave complacency behind, ask yourself a couple of questions:

1. Have I in any way adopted a theology of
   complacency?

2. Have I justified a life of complacency (as in just going to church and living a pretty good life)?

If either answer is *yes,* go back to the beginning. Rediscover the great treasure that He is. Desire more of His holy presence. Putting the flesh to death will make room for more of God in your life—and He will give you the power to be resilient.

BECOME RESILIENT

- If you give in to the theology of complacency, you will never make the mark on the world that God intended.

- Those eagerly pursuing the things of God are not being overly ambitious or works oriented. They have found a treasure they are willing to give up every-thing for—because nothing compares to it.

- You discover the treasure (that God sent His Son to bring us life) by His grace, and when you do, your heart cannot help but change. You become desperate for more of God and earnestly desire Him.

If at any point you justified a life of complacency, take this time to repent and rediscover the treasure God has given us.

Lord, I repent now for just going through the motions. I realize that the treasure is worth giving up everything for. I trade in my flesh, my will, my ways, my opinions for You, because nothing compares to You. Draw me close to You and change my heart by Your grace, in Jesus's name. Amen.

Real-Life Resilient: Rahim

An Iranian man in difficult circumstances found the ultimate treasure and has exchanged everything for it. At an early age Rahim lived on the streets and wanted nothing more than to leave his country. Believing that God had abandoned him, he turned away from God and toward witchcraft.

Rahim asked God why he felt ignored during his trial. After searching the Scriptures, Rahim realized that God had not deserted him. He chose to surrender his life fully to Christ by turning away from sin. But demonic spirits continued to torment him.

When Rahim was prayed for at a prayer meeting, his life was transformed. "I became free. It was suddenly like my eyes were open," Rahim said. "I did not even have the strength to think about anything. It was like I was seeing everything for the first time."

Rahim's priorities changed. Instead of wanting to flee Iran, he wanted only to follow Christ. Even when he was held in solitary confinement and heard his wife's cries coming from another cell, Rahim was thankful. "When they put me in the prison and shut the door, I just fell on my knees and kissed the ground. I said to God, 'You have got a purpose that we are here.'"[1]

A treasure, indeed!

Chapter 5

JESUS, THE LIFE-ENHANCEMENT DRUG

I N LIFE THERE are things that we need and things that we want. There is a big difference between the two but needs and wants are often confused. We say things like, "I *need* Starbucks right now" or "I *need* to get that new CD." But do we really need those things to survive? Or do we just want them?

When a wealthy man questioned Jesus about eternal life, Jesus highlighted the difference between the man's needs and wants:

> A certain ruler asked him, "Good teacher, what must I do to inherit eternal life?"
>
> "Why do you call me good?" Jesus answered. "No one is good—except God alone. You know the commandments: 'You shall not commit adultery, you shall not murder, you shall not steal, you shall not give false testimony, honor your father and mother.'"
>
> "All these I have kept since I was a boy," he said.
>
> When Jesus heard this, he said to him, "You still lack one thing. Sell everything you have and give to the poor, and you will have treasure in heaven. Then come, follow me."
>
> When he heard this, he became very sad, because he was very wealthy. Jesus looked at him and said, "How hard it is for the rich to enter the kingdom of God! Indeed, it is easier for a

camel to go through the eye of a needle than for someone who is rich to enter the kingdom of God."

—Luke 18:18–25

Like this rich young ruler, most of us have much more than we need. What we *need* is oxygen, water, and food. Needs such as these are obvious. But some needs are not as obvious, such as the need for love, relationships, forgiveness, and a connection with our Creator.

The things we want, however, are very obvious to us. Consider for a moment how you think about the things you want. What are you willing to do to get them? The person who wants a new car will work like crazy to buy one. The one who wants to be noticed by a certain someone will do almost anything to get that person's attention. We get passionate about the things we want, and we'll go crazy to get them.

I remember hearing about fathers in wartime Europe who actually stole food from orphans to feed their own children. They had never thought about committing such crimes before, but they were willing to do whatever it took to feed their children. That is what happens when you have a real need. You'll do whatever it takes.

To get a picture of a real need, imagine a drowning man. Can you see him clenching and clawing and fighting to get to the surface? A drowning man would fight with the last drop of his strength to get the air he needs. He is desperate to breathe. *Oxygen is not just a want; it is a life-or-death need.*

Needs or Wants?

We have all kinds of wants. We treat some of them casually and some with a sense of urgency. When the latest smartphone comes out, we might rush to be first in line, saying, "I've got to have that." We sacrifice our time and money because we want *that* phone and we want it *right away.*

Wanting things is not a problem (as long as you seek the kingdom first). Mistaking our wants for needs is a problem. It is important to understand what happens when needs and wants get confused. Say you have a car that really needs some help. It is rusted, the paint is peeling, and the tires are shot. The less discerning person might say, "I really need to get this car painted."

But should painting the car really be the top priority? No. What you really need are some new tires. Otherwise you'll have a newly painted car that won't go anywhere because the tires are bald or flat. Too often the preference is perceived as a need. Having the car painted is a preference. Making the car functional and safe is a need.

Failing to discern the difference between needs and wants causes us to make bad decisions. Imagine that you own several pairs of jeans but decide that you "need" some new ones. Meanwhile you have run out of groceries, but instead of buying the food you *need,* you buy the pants you *want.* So you go hungry until your next paycheck.

> If we perceive Jesus as a casual *want* who enhances our lives, we will never desperately pursue Him with all of our hearts.

The things we want are our preferences and desires. They add to our lives but aren't necessary for survival. They simply make life slightly more enjoyable. Needs are the things our lives require. There is an urgency for these things because we won't survive without them. Unfortunately too many people who call themselves Christians put Jesus in the first group. They say, "I need Him to get to heaven, but I don't really need Him to live each day. I have a pretty good life. I'm doing OK. But I'll add Him to my life because He makes it a little better." Jesus enhances their lives for all practical purposes.

For far too many people Jesus has become a life-enhancement drug. Sometimes this happens because of the way Jesus is presented to us. We hear things such as, "If you want that love, that peace, that joy in your heart…" Even though we're doing OK, we start thinking it might not be a bad idea to add Jesus to make our lives that much better. In many ways we become like the Hindus, who have more than three hundred million gods. If you don't explain Jesus to them correctly, they will say, "OK. I'll accept Jesus. I have all these other gods. Why not one more?"

Although we would probably never put it that way, that's how many Christians live. They add Jesus to their lives to make it just a little bit better. Here is the problem: if we perceive Jesus as a casual *want* who enhances our lives, we will never desperately pursue Him with all of our hearts.

In a wealthy culture such as ours it gets harder and harder to discern what our real needs are. Our lives get so full of life enhancements that we don't see what life is really all about. It's an advertiser's job to convince us that we need something when we really don't. So we end up thinking we need those shoes, that Wi-Fi, the latest gadget. We end up focusing on our wants while neglecting our needs. A teenager might say, "I need to spend time on the Internet," when what he really needs are real friends and not fake ones. A young girl might say, "I really need a boyfriend," when what she really needs is healthy affection from her father. A couple might say, "We need that expensive car," when what they really need is the approval of a loving God.

All too often we think we need what the culture says is important. So we fill our lives with "wants" because we've been told they will enhance our lives. We don't realize they are temporal and will burn one day. And then we add Jesus to that list of life enhancements.

How Bad Is the Problem?

When you know you have a problem and you understand its degree, your real need becomes clear. In the passage from Luke 18 Jesus tried to show the rich young ruler his need. The man said, "I've been doing all these rules since I was young. What else do I have to do to have eternal life?"

The man knew there was a problem, but he thought he could solve it by observing another rule. Jesus explained, "Rules aren't your problem. You don't need to add one little rule to your life. And you don't just add Me to enhance your life, either." Jesus did not die to merely enhance our lives and make them a little bit better. He did not die so we could add a little bit of Him to our lives like a woman applies makeup before she leaves her home. Jesus died to completely revolutionize our lives and change our total value system.

We can follow all the rules we want; we can be as good as we know how to be; but until we wake up to our most essential need, we remain lifeless and without the freedom that we desire. The sin issue is not just about the things we have done. The root problem is that we were born in sin. We are sinners because of what we are.

You can tell a dog not to bark, but he was born a dog, and dogs bark. You can tell a sinner not to sin, but he was born a sinner, and sinners sin.

People too often have looked at the world and said, "Just stop doing those bad things." How does that help them? They cannot stop. They were *born* that way. They were not born to bark, but they were born to sin. All of us were. We do bad things because we were born in sin.

Let's say we go to the doctor because we have a pain. We ask him how bad the situation is. What the doctor says determines how desperate we should be. The fact is, we were born with a condition so bad that no set of rules could take care of it. We don't need rules. We desperately need heart transplants. We may try to fix the symptoms, as so many people do, but fixing the symptoms never solves the sin problem.

We can't just decide to stop doing this or stop doing that or be a better person. Changing the heart fixes the problem. Jesus tells the rich young ruler, "Do all the rules you want, but they will never solve the root issue." This is why Jesus said we must be born again (John 3:3).

Too often in the Western world we try to fill our lives with enhancements that mask our pain. We are lonely, we are broken, we are filled with rage and hatred. So we take a drink or a drug. Or perhaps we watch television, drowning our sorrows and emptiness in entertainment. But what we really need is the grace and forgiveness of God. We need new hearts. We need to become brand-new people.

We are so up to our eyeballs in fulfilling our wants that we cannot even see what we need. Like the starving child with a bloated stomach, we are bloated but empty inside. We are fat with the things we want, but starving for the life of God inside us. If we realized the severity of our condition and the dire state of sin we were born into, it would produce in us a desperation for the nourishment we need—God Himself.

Jesus is the giver of life. Jesus did not die to be our life-enhancement drug. As a stillborn child is born physically dead, we were born spiritually dead. And just like that stillborn child, who cannot be revived no matter what the doctors and nurses do, only a miracle can give us life. This is how you and I were born: *we were born dead, and we needed a miracle.* Once we realize that you and I are the stillborn child—that we were born dead—then we wake up to the reality that we *need* life from Christ.

Our condition is spiritually life threatening. Imagine you were told you had cancer. It was disguised at first, so you didn't realize you had it. But over time it eats away at you, making you feel worse and worse until it slowly kills you. This is much like what happens to us spiritually. We were born with a spiritual cancer. Without the remedy of the Savior, the cancer slowly kills us. The trouble is that we don't realize it right away. Little by little the sickness eats away at us, so that we feel worse and worse. It is a miserable, tortured existence.

The cancer of our souls is sin. When you realize you have cancer you realize you *need* a miracle. That miracle called a new heart gets rid of the cancer of our soul! We *need* that miracle because we were born with this cancer called sin!

We are like people who grow up in internment camps and never know any other life. We are accustomed to the chains and grueling pain and think they are normal. What we really need is to be set free, but we don't realize it because we don't know what freedom is or what it looks like. So we settle for whatever enhancements we can find within the prison gates—a cup of coffee, an extra morsel of food, a better view of the outside world. These little pleasures don't meet our real need.

If you were born with a heart defect and needed a heart transplant, how ludicrous would it be for you go to a plastic surgeon to get a nose job? This is what it seems so many of us are preoccupied with doing. We care so much about satisfying our outward pleasures and desires that we pay no attention to the heart condition that is killing us. The heart defect is called sin, and the only way to get rid of it is through a heart transplant. When we realize the depth of the sin condition we were born into, we become desperate. We realize we *need* Jesus, and we want to do more than just acknowledge Him once during an altar call; we want more and more of Him each day. He is the very reason we are able to take another breath. When you realize you were born in this prison of sin, you know you *need* to be set free!

My guess is that Jesus is heartbroken by the limitations we accept. *Jesus did not die just to make our lives just a little bit better.* He did not die to just enhance our lives. He did not die so we could be a little more comfortable in our misery. He died to give us the life we desperately need. We must realize the seriousness of our condition.

When we realize we were born spiritually dead we will become desperate to pursue Him for who He is. We will realize the difference between our needs and our wants. What we really *need* is Jesus, not a life-enhancing drug. What we really need is Jesus, not something that makes our existence in this world a little more bearable. To become resilient, we need the Son of God to revolutionize our lives.

BECOME RESILIENT

- We must discern the difference between needs and wants. Wants enhance our lives; needs are those things necessary for our survival.

- Too often we think of Jesus as someone we add to our lives to make it better. But Jesus didn't die to enhance our lives; He died to transform our lives.

- More than anything we need to recognize how desperately we *need* Jesus. We were born in sin, and it is killing us. We need a heart transplant that only Jesus can give.

Don't let your wants blind you to your real need for Christ. Allow God to transform your heart. Ask Him now to fill you with His life.

Lord, I realize You died to do more than enhance my life. You died to revolutionize it. I repent now for any ways I saw You merely as someone who would make my life a little better. You are life itself. I need You. Transform my heart and change my life, in the name of Jesus. Amen.

PART 2

THE FOUNDATION OF RESILIENT FAITH

WHETHER TIMES ARE good or bad, sweet or raw, what we believe colors what we perceive—and *how* we believe determines what our faith produces.

Resilient faith is the kind that will sustain us for a lifetime. It is a faith that does not change with the weather or weaken when times get hard. Resilient faith holds up when hit by life's setbacks and curve balls. It chooses to follow the Savior *no matter what.*

Whether or not our experiences feel good, support our theology, complete our plans, or make sense to the natural mind, resilient faith holds steady. It is the kind of faith Jesus always meant for us to have.

However, it's not enough simply to talk about what resilient faith is; we must unearth what it is that produces resilient faith in our lives. What are the first steps in building that kind of faith? It does not come overnight. And when you find that you actually have resilient faith, it is not by accident. It all starts with the foundation.

We have examined several false and faulty foundations for many in the Western church. So what is the right foundation?

It begins with a paradigm. What is your frame of reference? How do you view the essence of God's interaction with man? Let's jump into a series of discussions that can frame our faith in a way that builds strength—because the way we see things changes everything.

Chapter 6

WHAT DOES IT MEAN TO FOLLOW?

NOW THAT WE have examined the somewhat unscriptural ways that people come to faith and the faulty foundations they produce, you may be wondering how Jesus expects us to connect with Him and with the Father.

A simple sentence explains a deep concept: "Follow Me." That is what Jesus said again and again. He chose to use the verb *follow* to describe how we initiate relationship with Him. Jesus said these two words over and over. They are among the ones He repeated most often throughout the Gospels of Matthew, Mark, Luke, and John. He was not being redundant. If this is one of the phrases Jesus repeated most, there must be reason He said "follow Me" so much.

Jesus told Peter and Andrew, "Follow Me, and I will make you fishers of men" (Matt. 4:19, NKJV). The brothers dropped their nets and followed Him. When another man wanted to bury his father and connect with Jesus afterward, the master said, "Follow Me, and let the dead bury their own dead" (Matt. 8:22, NKJV). When Jesus told Matthew, the tax collector, "Follow Me" (Matt. 9:9, NKJV), Matthew too dropped everything and followed Him, just as Peter and Andrew had done. On another occasion Jesus told His disciples, "If anyone desires to come after Me, let him deny himself, and take up his cross, and follow Me" (Matt. 16:24, NKJV).

That is a mouthful!

Jesus spelled out His requirements clearly: if we want to engage with Him and be His disciples, we have to follow Him. So what is this "following"? What does it mean to follow Him? How do we do it?

FOLLOWING IS A JOURNEY

In John chapter 3 Jesus said we must be born again. Please understand that being born again is *what happens* when you choose to follow Christ. You become a new person in Him. Following Him is not simply choosing to obey a bunch of rules; it is submitting yourself to His authority. It means saying, "I subject my mind, will, and emotions to Christ. I turn over my heart to Him. I give Him my past, present, and future. I want to bring all of myself under submission. I choose to deny myself."

I remember sitting with Oral Roberts at his home in California, asking him a standard question one might ask someone of his stature. But I receieved a totally unexpected response. "How have you stayed faithful to Jesus all these years and to your ministry and marital vows?" I queried. He paused for what seemed to be four to five minutes until it felt really awkward. I expected something such as "I read the Word and kept a consistent prayer life, etc." What he told me shocked me. He looked right into my eyes with steely conviction and said, "Ron, when I gave my life to the Lord at seventeen, I really gave my whole life to the Lord. I mean, I didn't just pray a prayer, I really got *saved!* I turned my whole life over to Him. He is my master." I felt tears welling up in my eyes as he spoke. I was thinking, "That's what happened to me. I gave my whole life too. I abandoned myself. I let go of control over my life!" It's as if he said, when you got saved *what kind of saved did you get?* Because I really got *saved* from this world and from sin!

Following Christ has many implications. For example, it means following His teachings and lifestyle. In coming to Christ we come to a fork in the road. We can choose to follow ourselves, our flesh, our friends, the culture, whatever is popular and convenient, and whatever lifestyle we already learned. Or when we are confronted with the opportunity to have a brand-new life in Him, we can begin following Him and living the life we were designed to live!

It all begins with a first step and a choice to walk in the right direction. When we pray to commit ourselves to Christ, the prayer is not what saves us. The prayer is the beginning of a new path. We choose to walk

> Following Him is not simply choosing to obey a bunch of rules; it is submitting yourself to His authority.

it because we choose to follow Him. The miracle of what happens is barely describable with words. The moment we decide to follow Christ is the moment we quit fighting with God. We stop saying, "I'm going to live my own life. I'm going to be a self-made person. I'm going to do as Frank Sinatra said and do things my own way."

Instead we choose His way. Yet it is just the beginning. The relationship requires interaction. We don't want to be like a husband who, five years into his marriage, hears his wife say, "Honey, you never say you love me anymore." Ten years later, she says, "Honey, you never say you love me anymore." In twenty years' time, nothing has changed, and she says the same thing, "Honey, you never say you love me anymore."

Finally the husband has had it. He puts his foot down and says, "I told you the day we married that I love you! If I change my mind, I'll let you know."

It seems that too many Western Christians are saying, "I prayed the prayer; leave me alone! I want to live my own life. I've signed on the dotted line, and I'm going to heaven. Get off my case!"

That is not the kind of relationship Jesus desires. In fact, it is not a relationship at all! He wants us to engage with Him every day. He wants us to have an everyday, ongoing relationship, and that looks like us consciously following Him day by day.

That first step in the right direction is great, but it is only the first step. There is another step to take the next day and another one the next day. Next week and next month there's another step. The adventure Christ has for us unfolds day by day, step by step. We keep walking with Christ and living with Him.

Following the Invisible, for Real

Some would ask, "How do you follow someone who's dead?" It is the wrong question. He is *not* dead. He's alive! The living God does not call you to follow a dead guy. When you choose to follow Jesus, He comes to live inside you! When He does, you will know just how alive He is.

A better question might be: "How do you follow someone who is invisible?" You cannot see Jesus with your eyes. He is not invisible, we just can't see Him right now. Just because your spouse goes into the other room does not mean she is invisible; she is just beyond the grasp of your eyes for the moment. But He is still real. Love is invisible but it's real. The human conscience is invisible but it's real.

Jesus is not visible right now, but He is real. One day you will see Him face to face and touch His scars, as Thomas did (John 20:27–28). You might even give Him a high five. And He will give you a bear hug!

Jesus really is the Son of God, and He has a real body. For now we cannot see it, but we believe anyhow and we follow Him. When Thomas touched His wounds and said, "My Lord and my God," Jesus said, "You only believe because you have seen; but blessed are those who believe without seeing" (see John 20:28–29). That is us!

Choosing to follow Christ means we do it even though we can't see Him. It is not as strange as it sounds. Do you follow any bands that you have never seen in person? Sure. You listen to their music.

You learn about them on the Internet. You might even memorize the lyrics to their songs. When someone says, "I love this band," you perk up and ask, "What do you think of this song?"

If the band is known for that song, you expect the person who loves the band to know it. If not, you suspect that he or she is not a real follower, but a "poser." A follower would *know* that song.

The same is true of those who follow Christ. They get to know His Word (His "lyrics"). When you follow somebody, you find out what they said. You find out what they wrote. You find out about their life. Ardent followers read Jesus's words and become familiar enough to share them with others. When someone is hurting or asks a question, the serious follower can say, "Here is what Jesus says about that." You know because that's what followers do—they know the One they follow.

What if we were such serious followers of Christ that we knew His opinions on just about any subject that might come up in the course of a day? What if we knew Jesus's "lyrics" better than we know all other lyrics? You may be thinking, "That's a lot of lyrics!"

Chances are you know more songs than you can name off the top of your head. You know them because you follow the artists. You are fervent about them. You *want* to know their songs, and you want to buy everything they release.

Here is my question: Is that how you follow Christ? Do you have the same passion for Him and His Word?

Too often we are like the poser who claims to follow a band, but does not even know the band's most popular song. We say, "I love Jesus." We know John 3:16 by heart, because we learned it when we were five years old. But we have not learned much Scripture since then. We claim to follow Him, but we take His "lyrics" for granted.

THE ULTIMATE KIND OF FOLLOWING

Really and truly, *followers follow.* They get to know the One they follow. They learn about His life. They become familiar with His teaching. They emulate His ways. They seek His heart and want to learn how He wants us to live.

Many people have a favorite college or professional sports team. They cheer for them at games. They know the players stats and how many times the team has been to the playoffs. They follow the team. They follow every game. This is what followers do—they know about the ones they follow even if they've never seen them face-to-face.

I believe Jesus is looking for a new generation of followers who don't just scream loudly at Christian events or speak perfect "Christianese." It is fine to say, "Praise the Lord. Glory to God. Hallelujah. Amen." But Jesus is looking for something deeper. He is looking for people who actually know the words of the Son of God they say they follow.

For too long faith in the church has grown weaker because we follow our favorite bands and sports teams more passionately than we follow the Savior of the world. We memorize songs and rattle off our teams' stats. We follow schedules and show up for events. Yet when it comes to Jesus, we barely make time to hear His voice.

What if we knew more about Jesus and His Word than we do about anything or anyone else? That is what true Christ followers do. They follow Him closely and take Him seriously. They don't need to be pumped or hyped up. They simply *follow.* They say: "I follow because I am a disciple. I am a learner; I am hungry to know the One I follow."

Here is how Jesus described it: "My sheep listen to my voice; I know them, and they *follow me*" (John 10:27). In other words, those who follow Jesus become familiar with His voice. They get to know His words, and they do what He says.

Jesus made it clear that *following* is not a menu option, but a requirement for those who call Him Savior. Jesus said, "If anyone serves Me, he must follow Me; and where I am, there My servant will be also" (John 12:26, NAS). As far as Jesus is concerned, we cannot serve Him without following His ways and His teachings.

The ultimate goal would be to follow Christ so closely that people mistake us for Him. That's how the believers were first called *Christians* in Antioch (see Acts 11:26). They didn't call themselves Christians; the secular people did. Those believers following the way did not look and act like Christ, they named them Christians, or "little Christs."

Someone would ask, "Is that Jesus?"

"No, that's Peter," was the answer.

"Wait—is *that* Jesus?"

"No, that's Mark," someone replied.

"Is that Jesus, over there?"

"No, that's Mary; but she looks and acts just like Jesus."

Whether male or female, these believers were so closely aligned with Jesus that they were mistaken for Him. No wonder the name *Christian* stuck.

Today people call themselves Christians, even when they don't live anything like Christ. What would happen if there were no difference between who we claimed to be and how we live? What would happen if Christianity got its reputation back? The greater question is: What if people truly saw Christ in us? Imagine if our lives caused them to say, "I've never met Christ personally, but I'll bet that is how He acts."

That is the true goal of our "followership."

MORE THAN WORDS

Please note that Jesus never asked anybody to become a Christian. For years now I have not done it, either. I don't ask people to become Christians, because I believe the goal is to become followers of

Christ who act like Him. When people see that, they will want to know Him. They will get their first glimpse of Him in us.

You already know that how we lead people to Christ is important because it affects how they walk out their faith. I mentioned in an earlier chapter that we would take a closer look at the verses we famously use as the capstone to the so-called Romans Road to salvation. Let's do that now:

> "The word is near you; it is in your mouth and in your heart," that is, the message concerning faith that we proclaim: If you declare with your mouth, "Jesus is Lord," and believe in your heart that God raised him from the dead, you will be saved. For it is with your heart that you believe and are justified, and it is with your mouth that you profess your faith and are saved.
> —ROMANS 10:8–10

We use this passage to explain how we become Christians. Sometimes verses sound so spiritual to us that we assume we know that they mean. But do we? This passage talks about declaring or *confessing* Jesus as Lord so that we can be saved. I believe we need to understand this in the larger context of Jesus's repeated command: "Follow Me." Confessing Jesus as Lord is more than just saying the words. Jesus Himself said "Not everyone who says to Me [or calls me], 'Lord, Lord,' shall enter the kingdom of heaven" (Matt. 7:21, NKJV.)

Christianity is not magic. We don't become followers of Christ by merely reciting certain words. Imagine if your faith were put on trial in a courtroom. The bailiff would put you under oath and the prosecutor would interrogate you. If he examined your lifestyle, would there be enough evidence that Jesus is your Lord to actually convict you? Would your actions and attitudes and lifestyle reveal that He is in charge of your life?

Of course, only God can judge the heart, but let this illustration paint a picture in your mind. I pray that as the prosecutor pressures you, asking, "Are you a follower of Christ? Is He in charge of your life? Is He your Lord?" you would cry out, "Yes! You got me—I confess! He is my Lord. He is in charge of my life. I follow Him with everything that I've got. I obey His Word; I listen to His teachings; I do everything I can to submit to Him! You're right, He is my Lord!"

I believe this is the true intent of the confession mentioned in Romans 10. It is about more than reciting a series of words; it is about confessing that Jesus really is in charge of your life.

There is another piece in Romans 10: believing that God raised Christ from the dead. This conviction comes from the Holy Spirit. He prompts us to believe. He woos us to believe. He opens our eyes so we see the truth. Because the Holy Spirit woos us, we say, "I believe!"

We embrace by faith a belief that Jesus died on the cross, that He rose again, and that He is alive today. We embrace the truth that He is the Savior of the world. When we believe that, He makes us righteous. He gives us new hearts and takes away the iniquity and shame and breathes in new life. With our mouths, we confess unto salvation. In other words because we confessed, because we said out loud, because we admitted, "Yes, He is my Savior! Yes, He is my boss! Yes, I am a follower of Christ," we are saved.

BECOME RESILIENT

- "Follow Me" is one of Jesus's most repeated phrases.
  That's because He wants us to follow Him. Jesus
  said, "If anyone serves Me, he must follow Me" (John
  12:26, NAS).

- True followers of Christ know His words and apply
  themselves to know all about the One they follow.

- Committing our lives to Christ is the beginning of a new path. We choose to walk it when we make the decision to follow Him.

Followers of Christ *follow*. If you have not committed to follow Christ or if you have wavered in that commitment, it's not too late to get on track. Let today mark your fork in the road. You can use the prayer as a guide:

Lord, I choose to follow You—period. You are the rightful owner of this universe and the rightful owner of my life. I will no longer pursue my own will and desires. I seek after You. I submit to You my mind, will, and emotions. I give You my heart, my past, my present, and my future. I commit to know Your Word and Your ways because that's what followers do. Help me to reflect You in all I do, in Jesus's name. Amen.

Chapter 7

CAPTURED BY CHRIST

P HRASES SUCH AS "I love you" are too flippantly thrown around in our common English vernacular. We say, "I love this hamburger," "I love this pizza," "I love your hair," "I love your clothes," "I love this car," and then, "I love Jesus!" That puts Jesus up there with the cheeseburgers. When we so flippantly throw the word *love* around, what it means to truly love God is easily lost.

If you were to ask most people, "Do you love God?" they would say, "Well, sure! I don't hate Him!" (That is, unless they truly do hate Him.) They would mean nothing close to what Jesus was talking about when He said, "Love the Lord your God with all your heart, with all your soul, with all your mind, and with all your strength" (Mark 12:30).

Instead of asking ourselves, "Do I love God?" a better question would be, "Has God captured my heart?"

Things that capture your heart grab your attention. My wife used to have this problem in the mall. She would walk by something that was staring at her from behind the glass, and it would capture her attention. She would have to go back into the store and put it on. She would model it and feel so good in it—even though she went in "just to see how it looks"—that before long she was walking out of the mall with it. She purchased the item because it captured her attention.

Movie trailers are good at doing this. You just see a two- to three-minute teaser trailer and it makes you want to see the whole film.

You can't think about anything else until the movie comes out. You keep looking at the website just to see when it is coming to your town. The movie has captured your attention.

Commercials are made to capture our attention and make our mouths water. That sizzling steak, that chocolate cake, that big-screen TV—they become all you can think about for the rest of the day. After seeing the commercial, all you want to do is get to that restaurant or to that certain store. It has captured your attention.

In order for us to have a firm foundation, we have to ask ourselves, "Has Jesus captured our hearts?" Have we been smitten with love for the One who gave His life for us? Or is He an afterthought, someone we acknowledge at the beginning and the end of our days? Do we see giving Him our time as an obligatory "something" to do so we don't feel like bad people? For us to be captured by Christ, we need to identify the things that have already captured us and taken the place in our hearts that should be occupied only by Christ.

Think about it for a moment. What has consumed your attention in the last day or two? What things steal your time and your focus? These things are competing with God for your full devotion. If God *really* is the great King of the universe who *really* gave His Son, then He is *really* worthy of all of our hearts.

JESUS WANTS OUR HEARTS

What does it mean to love God? Jesus said, "Love Him with all of your heart." The heart is the deepest part of who we are; it is our core; it is our center. Our love doesn't come from us; it comes from Him. He continually provokes us to love Him. God first loved us (1 John 4:19).

It turns out that the deepest part of our being is the first thing that God wants, and that is our hearts. *Our heart is the only thing that God really wants.* He doesn't care about our money; He doesn't care about our talents; He doesn't care about how our hair looks or how we dress. The thing He cares most about is not our performance for Him, or the rules that we obey. He wants us—the real us. He doesn't want an obligatory "Yes, I love You, Lord. Yes, I'll go to church. Yes, I'll do what You say." What Jesus does say is, "Those who love Me do what I command." (See John 14:15.) This is because those who obey Him do it out of a heart that has been captured.

After a man and a woman are married, they are smitten and enraptured with each other. You could say that they have been "captured by each other's love." They will bend over backward to make each other happy. Too often though, after a certain amount of time passes, what started out as joy continues as an obligation. There are too many people who live out their Christianity this way.

> What Jesus cares most about is not our performance for Him or the rules that we obey. He wants us—the real us.

Or imagine a husband who goes to work to get money to buy the food, to make the house payment, and to take care of the family. However, he does it out of obligation, not out of love or compassion. Imagine if a couple's marriage started off that way: They walk down the aisle and say their vows. But throughout all of it, the husband is only thinking of the benefits he is getting. He is getting a cook, a housecleaner, a sexual partner, and other perks. How crass it would be if his heart had never been captured by his bride.

That is how many people start their relationship with Christ. They think about what they are going to get out of it, but they never connect with the essence of what Jesus was after in the first place: their hearts. God longs to give us all of His benefits (see Psalm 8), but those benefits follow a heart and life that has been captured by Christ.

Loving With All of Our Souls

Our souls include our will and our emotions. Imagine choosing to love God with our wills and allowing our wills to be broken, so that we could truly say, "Not my will but Yours be done," as Jesus said in the Garden of Gethsemane.

As we have discussed before, loving with our emotions does not mean letting our emotions manipulate us. Instead, it means choosing to submit our emotions to the Word of God. It means deciding throughout the day which emotions are OK and which ones should be cast aside. For example, if you are living in fear, then you should cast the fear aside and put it in His hands. If you are living in anxiety, cast your anxiety unto Him.

Loving Him with our emotions also taps into this deep, emotional heart connection that He wants to have with us. We typically experience this emotional connection with the Lord most strongly when we worship. Sometimes walking into the middle of a service where people are worshipping with all of their hearts, souls, and emotions is like walking in on a couple when they're kissing. It's a little awkward because you feel like you are not supposed to be there.

Worship is the ultimate expression of our emotional connection with God. As we worship, we personally interface and draw near to Him.

Loving With All of Our Minds

What if we screened all our thoughts based on what honors God? Second Corinthians 10:5 says: "We demolish arguments and every pretension that sets itself up against the knowledge of God, and we take captive every thought to make it obedient to Christ." How we think, what we think about, the philosophy by which we live, what we listen to, and what we watch shapes us.

What would happen if we truly set our minds on the things

above? What if we had nothing to do with the "fruitless deeds" of the world (Eph. 5:11)? Our minds are the tool God has given to us to think, to build, to engineer, and to plan. Surely a mind that is set upon God is a mind that will accomplish the most for His kingdom. What if, instead of allowing our minds to become the playground of the enemy, it was a playground for God?

Love With All of Our Strength

"How do you love God with your strength?" You love Him by what you do each day. Your love is reflected in how you exert your energy, how you treat people, and how you interact with others. It is reflected in your college, your career, your future.

It is even reflected in team sports. It's very common for a coach to look a player right in the eye and say, "Are you giving me your all? Give me your all!" He is demanding, he is commanding, he is insisting that every bit of physical energy be exerted on the field or court at *that* moment. This is what Jesus is asking for when He says, "Love Me with your strength." He is saying, "Love Me with every ounce of your energy."

All too often our Christian service becomes obligation to a written set of rules. We need to go back to the title of this chapter and ask ourselves, "Has He captured my heart? Have I gotten rid of the things that so easily try to capture me on a daily basis? What things do I love and pursue?"

Jesus is inviting us to be in hot pursuit *of Him*. We know what pursuit looks like in earthly relationships. Something happens when a man pursues a woman. He pursues and pursues and pursues; he woos her heart and she responds. Praise be to God that He pursued and pursued and pursued us, and at some point we responded. The question is, have we continued to respond? The world keeps teasing us and trying to capture us with another preoccupation. They draw us in with another ad or another activity.

This is why Jesus said, "Seek Me *first*. Seek *first* the kingdom of God and all these things shall be added unto you" (Matt. 6:33). If we do this, our minds aren't focused on having the things. We remain captured by Him because we are seeking Him first.

A daily "heart check" would do us well. Ask yourself today: "Has my heart been captured by Christ?"

BECOME RESILIENT

- To truly love God is to have our hearts captured by Him. It means He has grabbed our attention above all else.

- The heart is the deepest part of us. It is the only thing we have that God really wants.

- Loving and serving God is about more than living up to a set of rules. We must love Him with all of our strength—with all that we do and all the energy we use to do it.

Lord, I choose to be captured by You. I want to love You the way You deserve to be loved. Teach me to love You with passion. Let Your pursuit of me compel my fierce pursuit of You. I give my attention to You and to the things that are important to You. I submit my heart, soul, mind, and strength to serving You, in Jesus's name. Amen.

Chapter 8

CHILDISH FAITH OR CHILDLIKE FAITH?

J
ESUS SAID, "UNLESS you...become like little children you will never enter the kingdom of heaven" (Matt. 18:3). He wasn't referring to *childish* faith; He was talking about *childlike* faith. One of the biggest signs of the former is what I call "easy believism." We have an epidemic of it. It has created a foundation in most people's faith that is not built on just sand, but on quicksand.

Let me explain. Jesus talked many times about having faith and about believing. The most famous scripture about believing is John 3:16: "For God so loved the world, that he gave his only son, that whoever *believes* in him shall not perish but have eternal life." We know this verse so well, but do we know what Jesus meant by the word *believe*?

For a fuller view let's note some other things Jesus said about believing. When the Jews sought to kill Him, Jesus spoke sharply about believing in Him: "Truly, truly, I say to you, whoever hears my word and believes him who sent me has eternal life. He does not come into judgment, but has passed from death to life" (John 5:24, ESV). When His followers wanted to know how to work the works of God, Jesus answered: "The work of God is this: to believe in the one he has sent" (John 6:29). When Lazarus's sister Martha grieved over her brother's death, Jesus challenged her belief. "Yes Lord," she replied, "I believe that you are the Messiah, the son of God, who is to come into the world" (John 11:27).

Jesus did not point to a childish, easy-believing faith. He made the seriousness of the issue plain. He showed His followers that believing had eternal implications and involved obedience. He minced no words.

The apostle John provided additional insights into the importance and purpose of believing:

> These [signs] are written that you may believe that Jesus is the Messiah, the Son of God, and that by believing you may have life in his name.
> —JOHN 20:31

> And this is *his command:* to believe in the name of his Son, Jesus Christ, and to love one another as he commanded us.
> —1 JOHN 3:23

Jesus did not suggest that we believe; He commanded us to believe. This is not about believing the sky is blue and leaves are green. That is easy; we *see* that the sky is blue and leaves are green. Too often we think we just need to get people to believe something and that saves them. We have all heard someone say, "I believe in God. I believe in Jesus. I guess I'm going to heaven." Is this what Jesus had in mind when He commanded us to believe? I think not. If you really believe something, you will do something about it.

Imagine a man is courting a young woman. What if in a moment of infatuation, he cried out, "I believe you're the one for me!" and then disappeared for a year? What if he returned only to repeat his strange behavior one year later, five years after that, and then ten years after that?

At some point that young lady is finally going to put her foot down, exasperated, and say, "If you really believe I'm the one for you, where's the rock? Show me the ring. You want to spend the rest of your life with me? Then do something about it. Make a commitment!"

When Jesus invites us to believe that He is the Son of God, our confession begins the journey. It is a step in the right direction, the first step toward becoming followers. But at some point we have to act on what we said. We have to believe to the point that we commit our lives and lifestyles to Him. We have to believe so strongly that He is the way, the truth, the life, and the only way to the Father, that we take His commands seriously. (John 14:6.) We have to believe so completely that we reorient our entire lives around Him.

What I mean is that we put Him in the center of all that concerns us. We determine that, from this moment on, everything—every friendship, activity, decision, and attitude—must revolve around Him.

Childish faith cannot do this. Instead it focuses on self and on what *I* want and need. Childlike faith steps outside of self and trusts in Him, wanting His will to be accomplished and making whatever commitment is necessary.

Another relationship example will help explain the kind of faith we need: What would be the point of my being married if I said to my wife, "It's really wonderful being married to you, but I want to keep my own apartment. You can keep yours too. It'll be great. We'll see each other every now and then."

What a broken-down, convoluted idea of sharing a life together that would be! When you marry, you commit and *reorient yourself* to a shared relationship. You decide where you will live *together.* You decide when to spend time *together.* You discuss decisions before you make them. You focus your life around the other person because you have made a commitment.

> Childish faith focuses on self and on what *I* want and need. Childlike faith steps outside of self and trusts in Him, wanting His will to be accomplished

That is what it means to make Jesus the center of our lives. It is not an expression of hyperbole. It is exactly accurate. He is the "sun" around which we orbit. We do everything in relationship to what He wants because we believe so strongly that He is the Son of God who gave us life. Because of that we owe Him all respect and honor.

We start with a simple, childlike faith that earnestly and eagerly believes whatever He says. We become completely dependent upon Him. That is what He wants. We are not to think that we can do anything on our own. Toddlers try doing that. They say, "No, I can do this myself." They want to be independent of their parents, even when they cannot possibly succeed without their parents' help.

Childish faith does the same thing. We think we are mature, and we quit depending on Him the way we once did. That is not His idea. He wants us to be like children who are utterly dependent on their parents for *everything*. That is the childlike faith God wants to see in us.

One final point is found in the following passage from one of Peter's epistles:

> For this very reason, make every effort to *add to your faith* goodness; and to goodness, knowledge; and to knowledge, self-control; and to self-control, perseverance; and to perseverance, godliness; and to godliness, mutual affection; and to mutual affection, love.
>
> —2 PETER 1:5–7

Our faith should be simple and childlike, yet Peter said we must *add to it*. In other words, we are to grow. This is not about works, but about our level of commitment to Christ. If we're serious about trusting Him, if we truly believe He is the way, if we follow Him with all our hearts, we can build our lives on a foundation of total and complete dependency.

Too many people who gave their lives to Christ when they were young never added to their faith. Ten, twenty, and even fifty years later they're still attending church regularly, but they haven't added to their faith. They haven't built a lifestyle of character. They haven't developed a lifestyle that is truly oriented around Christ. They have not yet made Christ the center of their lives. They still have the same habits they had early in their walk with the Lord, or even before they became Christians. They have not allowed Christ to deal with their anger, their financial decisions, or their relationships. They have settled for easy "believism." They are satisfied with a version of Christianity that says, "I believe in God. That is enough!"

Well, James 2:19 warns, "Even the demons believe…and shudder!" Having an oversimplified, childish believism is not a virtue. God wants us to have childlike faith that demands everything to be oriented around Christ. That kind of faith says, "I believe so strongly, I'll do whatever You ask, whenever You ask, even at the risk of my life. I'll do it even when I feel uncomfortable, or sick, or confused about what You mean. Even when I don't like what You ask, I will say, 'Yes,' because I am committed." Childlike, not childish, faith is what makes us resilient.

BECOME RESILIENT

- Childish faith focuses on self and what we want and need. Childlike faith depends on God like a child depends on his parents.

- God wants us to depend on Him for every need.

- It is not enough to just believe in God, we must believe so much that we are willing to follow Him anywhere.

- We must grow. We must add to our faith.

Lord, I won't settle for easy "believism." Yes, I believe in You, but I won't stop there. Jesus, be the center of my life. I'll do whatever You ask, whenever You ask. Even if I'm uncomfortable or confused, even if I don't like what You have to say, I commit to following You because I love You, in Jesus's name. Amen.

Chapter 9

GOD'S DYSFUNCTIONAL CHILDREN

IT SEEMS AS if everyone is talking about how dysfunctional their families are these days. Maybe there are no families without some degree of dysfunction. Even in the family of God many have a dysfunctional relationship with their Father. This dysfunction started way back in the beginning, the moment Adam and Eve, the first children in the family God created, attempted to live without Him.

Having the right understanding of our intended relationship to God is fundamental if we are to be resilient no matter what comes our way. Our Christianity is not something we strive for; it is a gift. God sent His Son to die for us, and by grace we are saved, not by our own works (Eph. 2:8–9). But the fact that we chose to follow Christ points to the reality that we once existed in this world without God and that He changed the essence of our existence when we found Him.

Jesus said in Matthew 18:3–4: "Truly I tell you, unless you change and become like little children, you will never enter the kingdom of heaven. Therefore, whoever takes the lowly position of this child is the greatest in the kingdom of heaven."

Look at the previous chapter and think about the difference between child*like* and child*ish* faith. Think about the attitude babies have toward their parents. They are completely, utterly, and totally dependent on their parents for food, for clothing, *for everything*. Something happens when children turn two, three, and four years old: they think they can fend for themselves. They try to act independently, even though there is no possible way they can survive without their parents' help and provision.

Interestingly enough we believers have some of the same habits as toddlers. After we have been in Christ for a little while, we think we can do things on our own. We begin to drift from the fully dependent attitude we had when we first came to Christ. Jesus had something to say about that attitude. He said those who are humble like children are the greatest in the kingdom (Matt. 18:4). Children know they need their parents for food and housing; they recognize the authority of their parents; they have a natural desire to please their parents; and they admire and respect their parents as heroes.

One of the foundational needs of children is love. A child without love dies both inside and out. This craving for love is common among all humans on the planet. We simply must have it. We cannot live without love anymore than a fish can live outside water. A human cannot live—*really live*—without love.

Isn't it interesting that God made us so that our greatest need (love) is the very thing He is made of! Scripture says that God *is* love (1 John 4:8). I wonder if that explains why we are so intrigued with love stories. The most popular tales and dramas for thousands of years have been love stories. The most common country, rap, and pop songs are all about love.

Symptoms of Life Without Love

It does not matter how many times our hearts have been broken; we always seek new love or more love. There is this thing that seems to elude us, a craving that is deep inside our souls. We want to have love, be loved, and love others. Love is the foundation for our lives, and until we experience true love we have never really lived. Children who don't know they are loved are maladjusted and dysfunctional. We have a whole world full of humans who, for the most part, don't know that they are loved by the God of the universe. And so we have all kinds of maladjustments, including wars, hatred, divorce, fighting, and hunger for power. These are all symptoms of an unfulfilled craving.

Let's look at some specific symptoms:

1. Failure to thrive syndrome

This happens most often in orphanages that have too many babies for the number of workers. The workers don't have time to pick up, hold, and love the babies. After months of not being touched, these children stop eating, stop growing, and stop smiling. They weigh less than normal and sometimes even die—simply from not being loved. It is not that they don't have enough food; they simply do not thrive. Imagine that—a baby dying from a lack of love. Many Christians are like this; they are failing to thrive. They do not know how much God loves them. They are trying to earn His love and provision. They are not growing; they are not smiling; they are not full of joy; they are not eating spiritually. They become listless and eventually dry up on the inside—just like an unloved baby.

2. Insecurity

Children who don't know they are loved grow up to be very insecure, always fishing for compliments. They ask questions such as: *How did I do? How do I look? How does my hair look? How are my clothes?* Sometimes their insecurity is expressed through arrogance; they overact in big ways because they don't want others to see their insecurity. Their cockiness is a symptom of not knowing they are fully known and fully loved.

3. Attention-seeking behaviors

Some children develop attention-seeking behaviors because they feel unloved. They often have negative attitudes, issues with drugs or rebellion, outbursts of anger, and bitterness. Many get piercings or tattoos or go from one boyfriend or girlfriend to another (particularly ones their parents don't approve of). Of course, adults have their own attention-seeking behaviors. The point is this: when you lack the security of knowing that you are loved no matter what, you unconsciously adopt behaviors you know will cause you to be noticed.

4. Earning approval

People who do not know they are loved try hard to earn the approval of others. Some do it by making good grades. Others strive to excel in sports. No matter how successful they are, some never feel they are good enough. They become legalistic about rules and regulations in their spiritual lives: *If I just do this or do that, God will approve of me more. He will love me more. I will be a better "toy soldier" for God.* They are trying to earn, earn, earn rather than just thrive in their walk with Him.

The biggest problem for people in this world is not knowing they are loved by the Creator of the universe. The biggest problem we believers have is not knowing how much we are loved by the Creator of the universe.

Live Like a Fish in Water

So what is the answer? Simply put, it is to live in God's love like a fish lives in water. Just think about it: fish are the last ones to realize what water feels like, because they are so used to being immersed in it. The idea of a fish living out of water is unimaginable. His gills are designed to take oxygen from the water. Take him out of the water and he flops around, gasping for air.

When my children were growing up, I would take them fishing. Sometimes we would catch fish, let them flop while we took them off the hook, and then throw them back in the water. Those flopping fish remind me of a lot of people, who were never meant to live outside of God's love. Most people do not live in God's love, so they flop around gasping for air and choking the whole time. The oxygen they long for is in the ocean of God's love.

God's dysfunctional children are God's love-starved children. When we are starved for love, we do all kinds of crazy things, and all kinds of dysfunctions develop in us. Once we understand that as humans we are designed to live in the ocean of God's love, we understand that there are also constraints in those waters. They are not hard, however. Jesus said, "My yoke is not heavy. My burden is light" (see Matt. 11:30).

His yoke is *not* heavy, but it is still a yoke. Our burden is this: to stay in the water, submerged in God's love. When we come to faith, there is a new King to whom we belong. There are new things to eat and new ways to live and relate to others (including parents, friends, and authorities). We now live in a completely new world, and we must learn a new lifestyle—the lifestyle of the King. This means doing what pleases Him. This is what it means to be a follower of Christ.

> God's dysfunctional children are God's love-starved children.

Many times people give their hearts to Christ but still want to live on land. But we have to learn to live in the kingdom of God, submerged in His love. Living in His kingdom is different from living on Planet Earth. We do not obey God's Word and live the way it says simply to fulfill an obligation. God doesn't want us to grunt our way along the path of life. We don't live in the ocean of God's love so we can breathe and merely exist. There are exploits to be accomplished and great adventures to experience. Following Christ is not just about survival.

Too often as followers of Christ we jump into the ocean of God's love excited that we have been born again. We have brand-new hearts; we have been forgiven; we swim around and have a great time because we realize that we *are* fish after all. We breathe in the oxygen of God's love and then look outside to see people on the shore laughing and smiling and partying and acting like everything is great.

We start getting jealous, so we jump back onto the land. We try to smoke and party and drink and sleep around or whatever, and realize after a while that we are gasping for air. We wonder why, but it is because we jumped out of the water we were meant to stay submerged in. People on the shore look like they are having fun, but they are all gasping too.

Then, when we are just about dead, we jump back in the water and repent: "Jesus, forgive us! Fill us with Your life. Fill us up with Your love again." Then we say, "It is so beautiful; He has forgiven me." But after a while we forget about the misery out on the bank, and we long for it again. So we jump back out of the water thinking we'll have fun for a while, until we find ourselves gasping for air again and jumping back into the water.

Our whole life is spent jumping in the water and out of the water over and over. It really doesn't make sense! Think about it. A beached whale is unnatural and so is a follower of Christ trying to live according to the world's rules. That is why it is time to jump into the deep and never come up.

This is what God is requiring. This is the most natural way for us to live: to dive into the deep things of God, realize that is where we were born to live, inhale His presence and His love, and learn to thrive in His kingdom with Him at the center of all that we do. We were created to operate on a whole different system from the world because we are not of the world. We just happen to live in it for now.

Learning to thrive submerged in God's love is the key to being resilient.

BECOME RESILIENT

- We were not created to be independent. We were created to be as dependent upon God as young children are dependent upon their parents.

- Telltale symptoms of insecurity surface when we are unsure that God loves us, but His love is more than enough to keep us secure. All we need is to realize how much He loves us.

- God longs for us to jump into the ocean of His love and stay there. Life on the shore is not nearly as good as it looks.

Lord, I am so grateful to be Your child, totally dependent and humble enough to see and understand Your kingdom. Thank You for loving me the way You do! Show me the depths of Your love. Help me to see not only that I am loved, but also how much I am loved. I choose to immerse myself in the ocean of Your love and to stay there. Fill me so full of Your presence that love spills over onto everyone I meet, so that they know You love them too, in Jesus's name. Amen.

Chapter 10

FULLY ALIVE

W ALKING THROUGH A store such as Hobby Lobby, you'll find an assortment of vines and plants that look remarkably like the real thing. Just look at the two plants pictured and see if you can identify which one is real and which is the imitation.

It can be hard to discern.[1] When I do this exercise in front of crowds and in various churches, the responses are usually at least fifty-fifty. But that means more than half of the people believe the fake plant is the real one.

Often, it *is* hard to tell the difference between the real thing and a fake. For example, those who forge paintings know that the better imitators they become the more cash they can make illegally.

Sometimes it can be hard to tell the difference between a real follower of Christ and a fake one, because on the outside they look very similar. It's a lot like the plants—some look alive, and some really *are* alive. The question is, how can you tell when something is fully alive?

There was a case of a thirteen-year-old girl in California who went to have her tonsils removed. Tragically she came out of this simple operation brain dead. Her mother refused to take her off life support, but instead went to court and got her daughter transferred to another hospital. The argument in the press was, "Is she alive or not? Does being brain dead mean she's really dead?"[2]

Just as this case made people think about what it means to be physically alive, I believe every would-be follower of Christ ought to think carefully about what it means to be spiritually alive. We should ask ourselves: "Am I alive, or am I just pretending that I'm alive? Am I fully alive in Christ? Am I doing the things that a truly alive person would do? Is my heart exploding with the life of God, or am I like a plastic replica of something alive?"

Interestingly Jesus brought this question to life in Matthew's Gospel:

> Just then a man came up to Jesus and asked, "Teacher, what good thing must I do to get eternal life?" "Why do you ask me about what is good?" Jesus replied. "There is only One who is good. If you want to enter life, keep the commandments." "Which ones?" he inquired. Jesus replied, "'You shall not murder, you shall not commit adultery, you shall not steal, you shall not give false testimony, honor your father and mother,' and 'love your neighbor as yourself.'" "All these I have kept," the young man said. "What do I still lack?" Jesus answered, "If you want to be perfect, go, sell your possessions and give to the poor, and you will have treasure in heaven.

Then come, follow me." When the young man heard this, he went away sad, because he had great wealth.

—MATTHEW 19:16-22

Be careful when you ask Jesus a question because, many times, He responds with the answer to a different question and makes you think about something you were not expecting. This man was asking the question that many people argue about today, both in Christianity and in other religions: "How do I get to heaven? How do I have eternal life?"

Jesus reframed the question. He essentially said, "Why are you only thinking about what happens after you die?" He said: "*If you want to enter life…*" In other words, "Why are you waiting until your death to find eternal life?" He forced the man to reckon with whether he was really alive or just existing.

Just because you exist on the planet doesn't mean you're alive or fully alive as God intended. Jesus's answer caused this man to look inside himself and say: "I know I'm here, but am I alive? Have I really entered life?"

Jesus said, "If you want to enter life" as though the young man was not alive yet. Jesus asked, "Why are you thinking about eternal life when you're not alive right now?"

Many people talk about how to get to heaven. They make the whole Christian movement about what happens when you die. Jesus is concerned about our becoming alive right now. *The best proof of eternal life is being fully alive right now.*

MAKING DEAD PEOPLE ALIVE

Too often we talk about all the bad things we do and about how we can be forgiven. All of that is important; however, the point is that *Jesus didn't come to make bad people good; He came to make dead people alive.*

The fact is that since Genesis chapter 2, all of humanity has been "born dead." God said to Adam and Eve, "In the day you eat from this tree you shall surely die" (see Gen. 2:17). So we think, "Well, Adam and Eve didn't die right then; they died later." But if you were to look into the reality of the situation, you would see that they died the moment they were separated from God. They existed after that, but they weren't fully alive as God intended.

When you are separated from God, you have the illusion of life without the experience of being fully alive. Just because you're breathing doesn't mean you're alive. It's amazing to think that you could have a pulse and still be dead, but that is what happened in the Fall. Adam and Eve died the very moment they ate of the wrong tree. The evidence of their death did not appear right away. They continued existing. They were like the plastic plant that looks alive but is dead on the inside.

Almost immediately after they sinned, Adam and Eve covered themselves with fig leaves. They knew something was wrong. Each of them thought, "I need to cover my shame. I need to do something to distract me from my deadness." They experienced the death of separation from God right away.

> Jesus didn't come to make bad people good; He came to make dead people alive.

It seems like much of our activity today is about pretending there's nothing wrong without God in our lives. We are trying to jazz up our plastic lives to make them look as good as we possibly can. After all, if we're going to live the imitation life, let's imitate as well as we possibly can, right? So we listen to the world's advice. The world tells us to eat this, watch this, smoke this, drink this, snort this, sleep with him, sleep with her, promising over and over that these things will give us life. But always, they give us death.

It's like we're eating candy that is poisoned. We keep trying new versions of the candy, but each has its own poison; each has a different way of distracting us from the fact that we are dead. This death entered the human race when Adam and Eve first sinned. It is still a bit of a mystery, because we think we're alive, but we are on the same quest as Adam and Eve were, trying every which way to experience life at its fullest. We might try adventure or thrill-seeking or money or a variety of romantic relationships, but none of those things can make us fully alive.

Second Thessalonians 2:7 calls this the "mystery of lawlessness" or the mystery of iniquity. We know that we are born in sin. We are conceived in iniquity as the psalmist says (Ps. 51:5). This word *iniquity* speaks of a twisted craving for evil and sin. Iniquity works inside us and causes us to crave things that are harmful. The mystery of iniquity is that it makes us think we are alive, even while it's killing us.

The voice says, "Just keep trying this. Just keep doing that," and all too often, we do! But if someone offered us rat poison, we wouldn't drink it and expect everything to be OK. Of course, the enemy disguises his poison with all kinds of sugar and spice. His poison seems good, even while it's killing us. The deceit of sin and iniquity says: "Eat this; it will comfort you. Watch this and be entertained. Smoke this and get high. Drink this to take the edge off. Do this other thing and be happy."

All are ploys that distract us from the fact that death is lurking on the inside of us. The distractions promise life, but they bring death. At the very best, they distract us from the fact that we are dead already and separated from God.

Jesus came to conquer death, hell, and the grave. (Hosea 13:14.) He didn't just come to conquer physical death; He came to conquer the death we are carrying around in us, this thing called iniquity that keeps lurking within. He came to give us life and life abundantly, as John 10:10 tells us. Jesus came to make dead people alive.

DEAD MEN WALKING

Most people are dead men walking, like prisoners on death row. When a person is sentenced to death and has been on death row a number of years, there comes a day when he or she heads for the death chamber. As the prisoner walks down the hall, the guards will shout, "Dead man walking!" Unfortunately that's what most of humanity is—dead men walking. They are trying to find an imitation of life to distract them from the reality that they are dead.

God is trying to keep us from living as zombies on this earth. *We are most fully alive when we are in communion with Him.* We are most alive when we are submitted, when we're dependent, and when we're connected. This is why God doesn't want us to sin. This is why Jesus taught us to pray, "Your kingdom come. Your will be done" (Matt. 6:10, NKJV), because when our lives are free from sin and entanglement, we're most fully alive.

When we commit our lives to Christ, He breathes life into our dead hearts. Then, in a world full of walking dead people, we become fully alive. As followers of Christ we ought to be the most alive thing our friends, neighbors, and coworkers have ever seen. When we walk in a room it should be as if life just burst forth. Why? Because we were dead but now we're alive. We were lost, but now we are found.

Paul explained the problem of death in Romans 8:13, where he said, "If you sin, you will die." He wasn't talking only about the law of sin and death (if you sin you'll die and go to hell). He was saying that when you participate in sin, the death you've been trying to outrun overtakes you, and you begin to just exist.

It seems this is the problem with too many who call themselves followers of Christ. They have had genuine Christ encounters in which their hearts come fully alive. But then they start tasting a little bit of sin here and a little bit there, and after a while something goes out.

When this happens, we become like light bulbs without electricity. We look the same, but there's no light coming through. We keep propping ourselves up saying, "I'm still a bulb; I'm still a bulb!" But there's no light shining. This is why so many Christians who say they are alive still feel dead. They go to church. They go through the motions. At one time they *were* fully alive, but now they sense deadness or a lack of authentic relationship.

Jesus said to pray every day, "Your kingdom come. Your will be done." In other words, we are saying, "I don't want iniquity to reign in me. I want Your kingdom and Your lordship to reign in me. I want to stay fully submitted, dependent upon, and connected to You." Maturity, then, is staying fully alive for longer and longer periods of time without iniquity dominating us.

Bruised for Our Iniquity

This mystery of iniquity still lurks within us. Jesus came to deal with the twisted craving for sin. In fact, if you look at Isaiah 53, it says He was wounded for our transgressions and bruised for our iniquity. When we think about how Jesus was brutally beaten, whipped, and tortured, we realize that He endured all of it and shed His physical blood so that we might be forgiven of our transgressions, our sins, the things we do outwardly.

But Jesus didn't come just to forgive us of the things we do. He came to deal with the root cause, which is iniquity. The root cause is what leads us to want to do bad things in the first place. The root cause is what provokes us to create some evil thing. The root cause is iniquity.

Isaiah's prophecy says that He was bruised for our iniquity (Isa. 53:5). When you get a bruise, the area often swells up. It may start out red and then turn purple because, essentially, a bruise is inward bleeding. Jesus was beaten externally and bled externally to forgive us of our external sins. But He was bruised internally and bled internally to deal with our internal human nature, the inner ways that need to be redeemed.

He dealt with our iniquity. So with every blow from the cat-o'-nine-tails, His skin was ripped away by pieces of glass and bone at the ends of the strands. But that was not all. There were also lead balls woven into the whip. They struck His torso, arms, and legs again and again. Every time those lead balls hit Him, He was bruised again to deal with our iniquity and to free us from the death lurking inside us. He did it so we could be fully alive—not just forgiven of what we did, but also freed from the root that caused us to crave the sin in the first place. That root is called *iniquity*.

Jesus wasn't just beaten, bludgeoned, and tortured. Many have endured that for all kinds of reasons. Jesus hung on the cross for six hours, and Isaiah said the Lord laid on Him the iniquity of us all (see Isa. 53:6). In the middle of all He suffered as part of His death sentence, God laid on Him the iniquity of every human, the thing that caused us to crave evil, including the evil thoughts that we are so ashamed of and would never tell anybody about. It includes that thing that was inside Hitler and Stalin—the thing that made them want to kill millions of people. It's that thing inside of drug lords today that causes them to want to sell drugs to children. It's the thing inside a crazed man who would kidnap teenage girls, fill them full of drugs, and sell them into prostitution.

What would cause all of that? It's called *iniquity*.

God laid on Jesus all our iniquity. In that moment He experienced something that you and I have experienced but He had never before experienced—the thing so bad that it put a wall between us and God. We know He already knows about it, but we are too ashamed to talk to Him about it. Yet we feel the wall between us and God. We know it's there.

Jesus experienced that for the very first time as iniquity was laid on Him, and He cried out, "My God, my God! Why have you forsaken me?" (Matt. 27:46; Ps. 22:1). He felt that wall for the very first time. He experienced death at that moment, separation from God on our behalf.

The point is this: As we daily surrender our hearts, our lives, and the propensity for iniquity that we're redeemed from, we need to remember to *constantly* surrender. That is when we have the greatest potential to live a life that is fully alive in Christ.

BECOME RESILIENT

- We need to check ourselves by asking, "Am I alive, or am I just pretending to be? Am I doing the things that a truly alive person would do? Is my heart exploding with the life of God?"

- Jesus invites us to enter into life now rather than waiting to enjoy eternal life only after death.

- The world offers distractions to take our minds off our "deadness," but if we will stay in communion with God, we will find healing and life.

- Jesus paid the price even for the iniquity that drives our sin. Our part is to surrender ourselves to Him.

Lord, I'm not satisfied with "looking alive"; I want to live fully alive in You. Please reveal any dead places and iniquity that build walls between us. I commit all of it to You, surrendering myself and embracing the life that was purchased for me, in Jesus's name. Amen.

Chapter 11

ONLY IF VS. EVEN IF FAITH

THERE ARE TWO sides of faith. The faith that Jesus woos us to is much deeper than the easy belief system that says, "I believe in Jesus" but doesn't truly follow Him. It is more than believing in mystical formulas that satisfy our every whim and smooth over every rough patch. The faith Jesus invites us to live is a journey that includes rough patches and difficult choices.

The latter is the faith recorded in Daniel chapter 3, where we find the famous story of Shadrach, Meshach, and Abednego. Although they lived in pagan Babylon, a nation that worshipped multiple gods, these Hebrew children loved the living God and refused to compromise their faith in Him. The king of Babylon was Nebuchadnezzar, who had built a golden statue of himself and ordered everyone to bow down and pay homage when certain music played. Of course, Shadrach, Meshach, and Abednego refused to honor an idol to any god or man, no matter the consequences.

And the consequences were great. The Hebrew children were brought before Nebuchadnezzar, who offered them one last chance to bow down when the music played. He warned that if they didn't, he would heat a furnace seven times hotter than usual and have them thrown into it. At this point you might think Shadrach, Meshach, and Abednego would have been intimidated. But despite the king's threat, they stood firm. Their response should cause even the faintest of heart to rise up with courage:

Shadrach, Meshach and Abednego replied to him, "King Nebuchadnezzar, we do not need to defend ourselves before you in this matter. If we are thrown into the blazing furnace, the God we serve *is able* to deliver us from it, and *he will* deliver us from Your Majesty's hand. But *even if* he does not, we want you to know, Your Majesty, that we will not serve your gods or worship the image of gold you have set up."

—DANIEL 3:16–18

Faith is like a coin with two sides. In verse 17 we see one side of faith. Shadrach, Meshach, and Abednego had confidence and were absolutely determined. They knew that God was *able* and *willing* to deliver them. So often when Christians pray, they waver between opposing beliefs. They say:

"Well, I know that God can heal me, but I'm not sure He wants to."

"God is able to put my marriage back together, but I'm not sure He wants to."

"I know God can reach my kids, but I'm not sure He wants to."

The Hebrew boys had no such doubts. They said, "God is able, and He will deliver us." They spoke with their shoulders back, their chins held high, knowing God was on their side. This is the kind of confidence we ought to have. This side of faith says, "God can and will deliver me. When we go to God in prayer for a financial need, a healing need, a relational issue, or on behalf of the nations, we ought to pray and ask without doubting. "Since we know he hears us when we make our requests, we also know that he will give us what we ask for" (1 John 5:15, NLT).

"I BELIEVE, BUT ONLY IF..."

This side of faith rests on the character of God. We know who He is. We know what His Word says. We know that He wants to heal, save, and deliver. The challenge with this side of faith is that we often add a whisper to it, a thought we'd probably never say out loud. We just live it out. This whisper sounds something like this: "God can and will answer my prayer. *And as long as He does,* I will continue following Him."

As I said, we would never say this, but it shows up in the way we act. We pray for something, fully expecting it to happen. But if somehow the prayer is not answered in the way we wanted it to be or when we wanted it to be, we become victims of feel-good faith. Our resilience caves in. The life is sucked out of us.

What we thought was strength and confidence was actually a conditional faith. Whether consciously or not, we tell God, "I will follow You, but only if certain conditions are met

"*Only if* my prayers are answered…

"*Only if* I feel good…

"*Only if* I don't face too many challenges…

"*Only if* everything is wonderful…"

It's as if we are singing a variation of James Brown's song: "I feel good, like a Christian should (*and as long as I keep feeling good, I'll keep acting like a Christian should).*"

Jesus encountered many people with this attitude. One said, "I will follow you, Lord; but first let me go back and say goodbye to my family" (Luke 9:61). "Another disciple said to him, 'Lord, first let me go and bury my father'" (Matt. 8:21).

These sound like reasonable requests. Why wouldn't Jesus let a person say good-bye to loved ones or bury his father? In the first example, Jesus said, "No one who puts a hand to the plow and looks back is fit for service in the kingdom of God" (Luke 9:62). In the second, He said, "Follow me, and let the dead bury their own dead" (Matt. 8:22).

Jesus was not being coldhearted. He was trying to communicate that those who are spiritually dead should take care of carnal things, and those who choose to be alive spiritually should simply follow Him. That is what it means to put your hand to the plow and not turn back. In other words, Jesus said, "If you are wrestling with this, if you're finding 'good reasons' for having second thoughts, you are not ready to come. If you think there is any good reason to not give everything and following Me with all of your heart, *then you don't understand who has invited you to follow.*"

Too often we turn our faith in God's provision into a weird Santa Claus story. We are like the child who sits on Santa's lap and begs for certain toys, but is disappointed when Christmas morning comes and he doesn't get everything he wants. Whether we do it subtly or overtly, we strike bargains with God. We pray, "Lord, if You get me out of this ticket, I will become a missionary in Africa." Or, "Lord, if You heal Aunt Suzie, I will go into the ministry and follow You with all my heart." Then when we get out of the ticket or Aunt Suzie is healed, we go on with life and forget our promise.

Even in these small ways, we are putting conditions on our following Christ. When God meets our conditions, we promise to stick with Him; when He doesn't answer when and how we want Him to, our passion wanes. We become less fervent in our pursuit of Him. Little by little we drift, and resilience fades.

It's this conditional following of Christ that is the real issue. If following Him is based on our conditions, what will we do when we face a real crisis? What happens when our prayer isn't answered right away? What if we started with a different premise? What if the premise of our faith was that *God is the rightful owner of the universe and the rightful owner of our lives.*

With that kind of foundation in place we could pray with confidence, knowing that He is a good God who wants to heal or deliver or answer our prayers. We would be satisfied to know that when and how He answers our prayers is up to Him and not us. We would stand up, whatever the challenge. This leads us to the other side of the coin.

I WILL FOLLOW *EVEN IF...*

The three Hebrew children from Daniel chapter 3 made a key statement during their trial. They said our God "will deliver us from the king's hand. But *even if* he does not, we want you to know, Your Majesty, that we will not serve your gods or worship the image of gold you have set up" (v. 18). What happened here amazes me. They walked through the fire with "even if" faith—*even if* everything came apart at the seams, even if they ended up in the fiery furnace, and even if they didn't understand, they would not bow down.

Some might say that the young men doubted God, because in one breath they said God will deliver us and in the next they said, "Even if God does not deliver us..." I disagree. Their words did not reveal doubt. *Their faith allowed for the mystery of God.* They knew no human could understand everything about God, yet they were confident that God could deliver them, and no matter what He chose to do, their faith in Him would not waver. They must have thought, "If for some reason we end up dying in the furnace and going to heaven, it won't be such a bad deal."

This *even if* faith is courageous. It has been the legacy of Christ followers from the beginning. *Even if* faith allows us to admit that we don't know (and don't have to know) everything. We sure would like to have a formula for everything that happens in life. We would like every circumstance to come with an explanation; but those are conditions. *Even if* faith takes all the conditions off. It says, "I'm going to follow Him no matter what. *Even if* that the person I'm praying for doesn't get healed, or

> If following Christ is based on our conditions, what will we do when we face a real crisis? What happens when our prayer isn't answered right away?

95

doesn't get healed instantly, I will follow Him. *Even if* something tragic happens that messes with my theology, I will follow Him."

That's what happened when Hannah crashed in the plane and four young men went to heaven. It flew in the face of my theology. Life hit me and my family squarely between the eyes. The evidence of our fallen world came crashing in around us. We were not the first followers of Christ to have such an experience, and we won't be the last. In those excruciating days we needed the attitude that said, *"Even if* we don't understand what has happened, we will still follow You."

First Corinthians 13:12 says: "For now we see through a glass, darkly; but then face to face: now I know in part; but then shall I know even as also I am known" (KJV). In other words, we understand many things, but they're not completely clear. We know a lot about the Lord, but we don't know everything. We would like to demystify the God whom we follow, but we cannot. He is the God of the universe, the Creator of all that is good; He made the heavens and the earth, and rescued us by sending His Son. We might like to know everything that is in His heart and mind, but we simply don't.

Only if faith is the opposite of *even if* faith. *Even if* faith says, "Even if there are circumstances I don't enjoy, I am going to follow. Even if someone I deeply admire lets me down, I'm going to follow. Even if a pastor or leader does something horrible, I'm going to follow God. Even if the person who led me to the Lord turns away from Christ, I'll follow Him. Even if the loved one I'm praying for doesn't get healed, God's already been so good to me, I'm still going to follow. Even if I never receive another answer to prayer for the rest of my life, I will follow the God who has already answered so many of my prayers. I'm still on the receiving end of this relationship, and I'm still going to follow Him."

Real-Life Resilient: Zhou Liang

When a young adult Bible study was raided by the authorities in Shandong, China, believers were taken into custody, and many of their families paid to have them released. The authorities banned the church's activities, but the pastor reported that the restrictions had the opposite effect: believers continued to gather, and new believers joined their ranks.

"Do they think the church is banned just because they say they ban it?'"Zhou said. "Who can fight the will of God? They did say they banned the church, but they couldn't do it. Now, we have more people than before."[1]

These believers would not be stopped. They chose to worship the Creator of the universe even if the massive power of the Chinese government was brought to bear against them.

FAITH THAT DOESN'T BOW

I remember visiting with Oral Roberts at his home in California before he went to be with Jesus. As we discussed this topic of faith, I was initially shocked when he held up his right hand and said: "Ron, I've prayed for millions of people with this hand. In those prayer lines, in those tents, literally millions of people I laid hands on—many of them were healed, but there were *many more* who weren't healed. We would see dramatic healings—people whose legs didn't work at all and they stood up and walked. But there were many more who didn't seem to have any manifestation of healing at all."

Oral continued: "Ron, I don't know why. I still had the same feeling of faith, the tingling in my hand, the same confidence as I prayed over these people. I don't understand why. But it didn't mean I would stop praying for the sick, because I know that God wants to heal the sick. So I just kept laying my hands on others."

As I listened to him I thought, "*This is the kind of confidence we must have in our God.*"

Like Oral Roberts, we know what His will is, so we pray accordingly, but we don't let the results affect us. We don't let them determine whether or not we keep going, because if we did, we would be putting conditions on our God. *Even if* faith is the faith Jesus intended for us from the very beginning. It is the only kind of faith that bears up under our struggles. It is strong because it chooses to put confidence in the character of God even when we don't understand our circumstances. It says, "I know He is good even when I don't feel good."

Struggles *will* come. Everyone knows somebody who has died prematurely. Too many people have been in horrible accidents that have left them maimed for life. When things like this happen, we ask the almost inevitable question: "Why?"

Through all the months of Hannah's recovery—the operations and physical therapy and adjusting to her new world—that is the question that persisted: *Why?* Why would God allow such a seemingly senseless tragedy? Why would He allow these four young men, who were passionate about serving Him, to die? Why would He allow my daughter to endure such pain physically, emotionally, and mentally? Why do bad things happen to good people?

When Katie and I found ourselves in the middle of a tragedy, we could not answer the *why* question. We knew we had to focus on what we knew instead of what we did not or could not know. We knew that Jesus loved us. We knew that He came and gave His life for us. We knew that He rose again. We knew He would come back for us, and we knew we would be with Him forever and ever.

Instead of focusing on the questions we could not answer, instead of focusing on explaining the unexplainable, we focused on the goodness of God. All the rest we left in His hands. We decided we were OK with not having all the answers. And somehow, focusing on what we did know assuaged the lingering pain of what we didn't know.

A lot of people will try to offer explanations about why bad things happen to godly people, and they often have good intentions and good theology. I understand wanting desperately to find the good in terrible situations. But I know that there are a lot of people who experience tragedy and may never understand why. Still, they stand strong in their faith. So must we.

Jesus has invited us to follow Him with all of our hearts, souls, minds, and strength. He asks us to trust Him even when we don't understand. He urges us to have so much confidence in Him that even when life seems to spin out of control—even if we end up in a furnace seven times hotter than anything ever experienced—we will not bow down. We will not change our behavior. We will not stop following the only One who is worthy of all we have and all we are. By His grace, we choose *even if* faith.

BECOME RESILIENT

- *Only if* faith is conditional. It says, "God can and will answer my prayer. *And as long as He does,* I will continue following Him."

- *Even if* faith says, "Even if I don't understand, even if there are circumstances I don't enjoy, I'm going to follow You."

- God wants us to place our confidence in His character, even when we don't understand our circumstances.

Lord, I repent for any ways I have put conditions on my faith in You. I put my confidence in Your character, and I will trust You whether or not my circumstances make sense to me.

I will not follow You only when things are wonderful or if You respond to my prayers the way I want. Like Shadrach, Meshach, and Abednego, I choose to walk in "even if" faith. Whether I feel good or not, I will not stop following You. I will remain steadfast, because You've been so good to me. You deserve my complete devotion, in Jesus's name. Amen.

Chapter 12

A NEW KIND OF RELATIONSHIP

WE USUALLY DON'T think very much or very deeply about the kinds of relationships we have with people. If we hope to be resilient in times of trouble and grow in our walk with God, we need to know that the nature of the relationship God wants to have with us is fundamentally different from any we could possibly conceive without Him.

With God, it is about covenant. But because the word *covenant* is so rarely used and is often misunderstood in our culture, we must learn more, until we understand the kind of relationship He desires and how different it is from all other relationships. Knowing these things will set a foundation in our lives for long-term strength in Christ.

TYPES OF RELATIONSHIPS

We have all kinds of relationships in our lives, but they boil down to a handful of types. Let's take a look at what they are and how they work.

Convenient relationships

Most modern relationships are born out of convenience. They often involve people in proximity to us—someone who sits next to us in math class or works in the next cubicle or shares the pew with us at church. We go to lunch with certain people over and over and sit in meetings with them day after day.

Convenient relationships aren't ones we seek out; they are more accidental. Yet all too often our friendships are established this way. We are not always proactive in finding the right kinds of friends. We end up with "convenient friends" who cannot really help us to grow in our faith or in our character for God.

Many romances today are built from convenient relationships. People have romantic feelings followed by convenient sex. They move in together because it costs less to have a roommate than to live alone. Little thought is put into these relationships. People tend to think only about how easy it is to function in them.

Sometimes our relationship with God becomes a convenient relationship. I might get into trouble and pray an emergency prayer. Or I might get pulled over and pray that God will get me out of a ticket. Maybe I have trouble with a child or some other situation, and God is the convenient place to turn for help.

This approach to relationship is so common. People accept Grammy Awards for songs with horrible, explicit lyrics and then thank God for His help in winning the award. God never intended for our relationship with Him to be one of convience when we get in trouble. He wanted something so much deeper than that.

Consumer relationships

Consumer relationships are transactional in nature. I drive to the gas station to buy some fuel and a Diet Coke. I have no deep, abiding commitment to the person at the checkout. I simply go wherever I get the best deal. When I order a latte at Starbucks, it's not because I feel committed to a particular Starbucks store. I might go to a different location next time. Because the relationship is transactional, I feel under no obligation to keep going back, either. If I find another deal somewhere else, then I'll go there. When I'm in a consumer relationship, I shop around for the offer that benefits me most.

Our lives are full of consumer relationships. The challenge comes when we allow consumer relationships to bleed into other, more important relationships. For instance, if a romantic or marriage relationship is based on consumerism (as so many are), we stay in it only as long as we feel we are getting something out of it. When the perceived benefit ends, we go somewhere else and feel justified doing it! We say, "You are not giving me what I need." That is a consumer mind-set.

Too many people have what is called "consumer sex." They say, "I'll have sex with you as long as I get my emotional needs met. But as soon as you stop meeting them, I'll shop around and find someone who makes me feel better about myself."

Sometimes our relationship with God is on the level of a consumer relationship. We come to Him to get whatever we need. When we stop getting it, we quit coming to Him. We say, "I'm going to stop praying. When He stops meeting my emotional and physical needs, I'll go somewhere else."

How often have we heard people say, "We come to God to get our needs met"? But God is looking for much more than a consumer relationship.

Contractual relationships

Deep contractual relationships are a little more intense than the others we have discussed so far. In the old days people could shake hands on a deal. Their word was as good as a contract. Nowadays dishonesty and distrust make contracts necessary for almost every business relationship. (Even many marriages begin with prenuptial agreements.)

It seems that most contracts are written to tell us what to do when the other party fails to keep their word and their commitment. The contract explains what happens when the thing goes wrong. Contracts essentially say, "I'll do for you as long as you do for me. I'll do this if you do that." Most consumer relationships now have a contract attached to them, which makes them more binding.

Sometimes we mistake our relationship with God for a contractual relationship. "I'll do this, God, if You do this for me. I'll pray this prayer, and You will take me to heaven. If I do this good deed, then You will reward me for it."

God has something much deeper in mind than a contractual relationship.

Covenant relationships

Covenant relationships are something completely different and worth exploring to see what they are all about. It is not really a combination of the previous three we have discussed; it is very different in nature. It binds the strength of the law with a very intimate and personal love relationship. It is more personal than a legal contractual relationship and more binding than simple feelings of love for another person. A covenant relationship says, "I'll do this for you, even if you don't do something for me."

We see covenant relationships between parents and children, for example. Every parent knows what it is like to have kids who sometimes misbehave. But even when they misbehave, the commitment remains: "I'm still your parent, no matter what you do or say."

If teenagers turn rebellious, the most challenging part can be the inexplicable love a parent has—even when in-your-face rebellion comes from the ones they coddled and nurtured and heard take their first breath. The parent's heart says, "It doesn't matter what you do to me or what you give back to me. I'm still yours."

From their earliest years children really can't give anything back to their parents. They can't pay rent. They can't mow the lawn. They can't do the dishes. They can't do anything but smile and giggle. But that doesn't diminish the parents' commitment or love, because they have a covenant relationship: "This is my little one who I brought into the world."

Incidentally covenant relationship is the only kind God ever mentioned having with a human. There was the covenant with Abraham and the covenants with Isaac and Jacob. There was the Mosaic covenant. From its very beginning the covenant with David was a very different kind of relationship.

Sometimes people say, "Well, my relationship with God is a very personal relationship." Those are usually the words of people who want deep, personal interaction but don't want any structure or accountability in their relationship with God. It is love without law. They want the mushy, spiritual, personal side where God is belittled by more convenience than covenant.

Let's take a look at God's covenant with Abraham. It is described in the Book of Genesis:

> So the Lord said to him, "Bring me a heifer, a goat and a ram, each three years old, along with a dove and a young pigeon." Abram brought all these to him, cut them in two and arranged the halves opposite each other; the birds, however, he did not cut in half....When the sun had set and darkness had fallen, a smoking firepot with a blazing torch appeared and passed between the pieces. On that day the Lord made a covenant with Abram and said, "To your descendants I give this land, from the Wadi of Egypt to the great river, the Euphrates— the land of the Kenites, Kenizzites, Kadmonites, Hittites, Perizzites, Rephaites, Amorites, Canaanites, Girgashites and Jebusites."
> —GENESIS 15:9–10, 17–21

This ritual sounds very strange to us today, but to Abraham, it would have sounded normal. Covenant relationships were the cultural norm. So when God laid out the plan for this covenant ritual, Abraham would have been familiar with it.

Even today in Middle Eastern countries covenant relationships in marriage are very normal. During the marriage ceremony

Bedouin tribes do something that is deeply meaningful but could be described as barbaric. At some point in the ceremony an animal, such as a sheep or a goat, is cut completely in half and laid wide open. The blood from the animal runs to either side. On one side the bride stands with her family, and on the other side the groom stands with his toes in the blood and all of his family behind him. As he stands in the blood, he makes a pledge to his bride and his family: "I will keep my word and my commitment to my bride and to this family. And if I don't keep my word, may I be cut in two and mutilated as this animal is."

The bride follows suit on the other side of the animal, with her toes in the blood as she says, "If I don't demonstrate myself to be a faithful wife all of my life, and keep my word, may I be as this animal, cut in two and destroyed."

Next the father of the groom stands in the blood and says, "If my son does not keep his word to be faithful to your daughter, may I and my family be cut in two and destroyed."

Then the father of the bride steps into the blood and says, "If my daughter does not remain faithful to this covenant and keep her commitment, may I and my family be cut in two."

This is how the marriage covenant is formed. It is far more meaningful than the words "till death us do part" from our modern ceremonies. In some ceremonies today there is no such commitment at all. Instead of vowing "till death us do part," the bride and groom commit to being together "as long as our love shall last."

Unfortunately this is how too many Christians perceive their commitment to Christ: "As long as my love shall last; as long as I'm feeling something good." That's a far cry from covenant.

THE MAKING OF ABRAHAM'S COVENANT

In the previous passage from Genesis chapter 15, we saw the ritual of making covenant. Two important things happened that we should note.

First of all, after Abraham cut the animal, he waited for the covenant to be finalized. Typically when a lesser servant made a covenant with the owner of the land, the lesser servant was asked to walk through the remains of the hewn animal, saying, "If I don't keep my word to you, may I be like this animal." In that way, the owner of the land heard the person's pledge to pay their debt or do whatever the commitment involved.

So, as Abraham cut the animal open and sat waiting until dark, he listened for the next instruction. He assumed that he was going to have to pass through the animal carcasses. Of course, the entire ritual was based on his question to God: "How do I know that You will bless me?" (See Genesis 15:8.) God responded, "Just bring me the animals."

Abraham cut all except the birds. He had to pledge something to God. Yet as he waited and waited, he got a surprise: God showed up with a flame of fire, and *He* passed through the pieces of the slain animals. This must have shocked Abraham. Essentially God was saying, "If I don't keep My part of this covenant to bless you, then may I die and be cut into pieces and be slain." God was promising to be torn into pieces if He did not do His part to bless Abraham!

Another thing must have shocked Abraham: the fact that he was not required to pass through the animals and their blood. As we just noted, the bride and groom would pass through to signify an equal commitment. But God was not willing to ask Abraham to make a covenant that he knew he could not keep. It is as though God was willing to pass through for the both of them.

What He was essentially saying was, "Not only will I be torn to pieces if I don't keep My word; but I will also be torn to pieces and killed if you don't keep your side of the covenant."

And He was.

Hundreds of years later, Jesus, God in the flesh, hanged on the cross. He was and beaten and crucified because Abraham and all of us failed to keep our part.

On the cross, Jesus fulfilled the curse of the covenant. Galatians 3:13–14 talks about this. It says that He became a curse for us so that we might receive the blessing promised to Abraham, and so that we might love unconditionally.

The point is that a fundamental understanding of what it means to be in covenant changes our lives. It is so important for us to understand the deep embracing of God in a covenant relationship versus a convenient, consumer, or contractual relationship.

In describing covenant relationship, Dr. Tim Keller of Redeemer Presbyterian Church says that understanding this leads to paradoxical obedience.[1] What he means is that the law of God is the condition of the covenant. We take obedience seriously. With all of our might we try to obey because of what it cost Jesus on the cross. With all of our might we resist sin like crazy.

Which leads us to the second item to note about God's covenant with Abraham: when we do fall, we can find our way back to God because there is no condemnation for those who are in Christ Jesus (Rom. 8:1). This keeps us out of a works mentality but also out of a cheap-grace mentality.

Jesus left His disciples with a sense of the covenant He was about to establish by way of the cross:

> And when he had given thanks, he broke it [the bread] and said, "This is my body which is for you; do this in remembrance of me." In the same way, after supper he took the cup,

saying, "This cup is the new covenant in my blood; do this, whenever you drink it, in remembrance of me."
—1 Corinthians 11:24–25

Describing the Last Supper, Jesus said, "I give you a new covenant." It's always been about covenant relationship. It is what God has always wanted for us from the very beginning. It's what He wants right now. It's a new covenant with His blood. In fact, He said every time we eat the bread and drink the cup in remembrance of Him, we would remember that He died and shed His blood for us.

It is a binding, intense covenant relationship unlike any other relationship that a human being can have with anyone else in life. My hope is that each time we take communion from now on, we take that bread in our mouths and remember that His body really was broken. And each time we take the cup, I pray we would realize that His blood was literally shed for us. He paid the price because we couldn't keep our side of the covenant.

> On the cross, Jesus...became a curse for us so that we might receive the blessing promised to Abraham, and so that we might love unconditionally.

Each time we take communion, may we feel the binding nature of the love of God drawing us closer— and in that reality find the strength to be resilient.

BECOME RESILIENT

- Understanding the nature of our relationship with God is critical to a foundation of long-term strength in Christ.

- The world's relationships of convenience, consumerism, and contracts are nothing like true covenant relationship God, which is so strong it binds both parties to the death.

- God knew we could not keep our end of the covenant. He covered His side of it and ours by dying on the cross.

Lord, I repent for any ways I have underestimated or misunderstood the covenant You have established with Your children. Worldly kinds of relationships are so shallow and self-centered compared to the relationship You have prepared for us. Your covenant sustains me and teaches me Your ways. Please reveal to me the beauty of Your covenant and of the love it represents. Thank You for it and for the price that You paid, in Jesus's name. Amen.

Chapter 13

WHAT TO DO WHEN YOU DON'T UNDERSTAND

J ESUS DREW MANY crowds during His three-and-a-half years of earthly ministry. Often He shared parables that seemed entertaining but carried powerful messages He wanted the throngs to grasp. Jesus was always trying to illuminate the nature of His Father and reveal the kind of relationship He wanted with His followers. Some understood and some did not.

Just as is true in the church today, some people listened to Jesus because they valued the entertainment of the parables more than the meaning. Others came to Him to experience the shock of seeing the blind healed and the lame walk. It seems humanity has always been attracted to the spectacular and supernatural.

MIRACLES DON'T NECESSARILY PRODUCE FAITH

One of the most spectacular miracles was the feeding of the five thousand in John chapter 6. For a long time I struggled to understand what Jesus said after the event. Having crossed the Sea of Galilee to Capernaum, He found more crowds waiting for Him. I think it is particularly noteworthy that in John 6:26 He said, "You are looking for me, not because you saw the signs I performed but because you ate the loaves and had your fill."

In other words, He was saying: "*You look for Me because of what you can get. Something supernatural is going on here, and you're not interested in or inquiring about what you witnessed—a miraculous invasion of God in man's affairs. All you really want is more free food."*

This started a series of questions followed by rebukes from Jesus. In one of the least entertaining teachings of all, Jesus responded to the question, "What sign will You give us that we may believe what You do?" (see John 6:30). It seems unbelievable that anyone would ask such a thing after the fish and loaves were multiplied. Yet the people essentially asked to see just one more miracle, so they could believe.

I think it's interesting to note here that some people say *a miracle settles the issue.* This idea assumes that if God does a miracle, people will be persuaded to believe. That is fundamentally untrue. Miracles cause *some* people to believe, but those people tend to be predisposed to having faith. In this case they had seen miracles and yet were still unbelieving. Many see miracles and still do not believe.

What we believe influences how we perceive things. If a person thinks there is no way God sent His Son to die for humanity or that there is no living God who performs miracles today, it doesn't matter how many miracles he sees. He will find a way to excuse them away.

That's what the Pharisees were doing. Jesus was not about to do a bunch more miracles to convince these cynics to believe. When they rambled on about how their ancestors ate manna in the wilderness, Jesus was on to them. He turned their rant around to explain that He was indeed the "true bread from heaven" and "the bread of life" (John 6:33, 35).

They replied, "Lord, give us this bread, always" (John 6:34, NKJV). The implication seems to be: "If You give us this bread, *then* we will believe."

Jesus rebuked them, saying, "But you have seen Me, and you still don't believe" (see John 6:36).

Hence my point that what you believe interprets what you see. What you believe can even prevent you from seeing something that happens before your very eyes!

I recently visited the synagogue ruins in Capernaum where Jesus preached this very sermon. I imagined all the people crammed into the very beautiful, ornate structure with its pillars and carvings, listening to the Messiah and becoming offended by His claims:

> The Jews there began to grumble about him because he said, "I am the bread that came down from heaven." They said, "Is this not Jesus, the son of Joseph, whose father and mother we know? How can he now say, 'I came down from heaven'?"
>
> —John 6:41–42

Jesus begins His message by saying, "I am the bread that came down from heaven," and immediately they start grumbling. "Wait a minute," they protested. "We know Him. Who does He think He is?"

It is the kind of grumbling you hear when people encounter teachings or circumstances that don't fit their paradigms. Jesus knew that the problem was their lack of understanding. "Stop grumbling among yourselves," Jesus answered. "None can come to me unless the Father who sent me draws them" (John 6:44). Jesus is leaning in a little bit harder to help them see the supernatural connection. The Father would have to draw them. Only He could illuminate their hearts.

No Watering Down

Please understand that Jesus did not try to make people happy. He did not soften His message so people would have an easier time believing it. He simply told the truth: they could not understand what He was saying unless God drew them.

I cannot tell you how many times I have stood before thousands of young people and asked God to draw their hearts toward Him. It is so tempting as a pastor or a preacher to soften the message in the hopes that people will come forward. It is daunting to know that people's whole spiritual futures can be affected by their response to the words you speak and by whether they believe and act upon the message you share.

I have said countless times that I would rather have one person fully surrender his or her life to Christ than have one thousand rave about a nice spiritual moment and a few goose bumps, without giving themselves to Him completely.

Based on the Scriptures, I believe Jesus felt the same way. In John's Gospel, He said something that seemed designed to push people over the edge: "I am the living bread that came down from heaven. Whoever eats this bread will live forever. This bread is my flesh, which I will give for the life of the world" (John 6:51).

The statement was raw and so provoked people that many apparently reached their limit. They'd had too much. "Then the Jews began to argue sharply among themselves, 'How can this man give us his flesh to eat?'" (v. 52). Essentially what they are saying is, "Does this man expect us to be cannibals? Does He really expect us to eat His flesh? How can He possibly think we would consider doing that?"

Jesus did not reach out and say, "No, listen, that was just a metaphor. Let Me explain what I really meant."

Instead, He continued to reveal truth, even as they continued down the path of skepticism:

> Whoever eats my flesh and drinks my blood has eternal life,
> and I will raise them up at the last day. For my flesh is real

food and my blood is real drink. Whoever eats my flesh and drinks my blood remains in me, and I in them.

—JOHN 6:54–56

Jesus's words challenged His hearers. "Many of his disciples said, 'This is a hard teaching. Who can accept it?'" (v. 60). They tried to wrap their minds around what He said.

Jesus knew that even His followers were complaining. He asked, "Does this offend you? Then what if you see the Son of Man ascend to where he was before!" (vv. 61–62).

We might paraphrase Jesus's response this way: "You're upset because you don't understand this? How about I fly up to heaven and come back real quick? Will you believe then? Will that lend more authority to My words? You guys just came out for more free food, but I am giving you something better—some real truth. You don't want to hear that. You want the spectacular. You want Me to somehow prove that I am who I say I am."

At this point Jesus reminded them that no one could come to Him unless the Father enabled them (v. 65). That was when "many of his disciples turned back and no longer followed him" (v. 66).

There comes a point when we stare in the face of circumstances that grieve us, or theology that does not match our experience and we have a decision to make. We are all tempted to give up as these did. The question is, will we walk out on God just because we don't happen to see the big picture? Will we walk away just because He did not answer a prayer? I heard someone say, "God answers every single one of our prayers exactly the way you would want Him to if you could see the big picture as He does."

I remember in the first few days following Hannah's accident we were confronted with circumstances that simply did not reckon with our faith. As I traveled to all four funerals of the young men who perished, it was a choice to believe the best about the nature of God. I had to choose to trust in His character because I know

He is good despite the inexplicable tragedy. After all, if God was passing out miracles that day, why couldn't all five survive? As I wrestled in my mind with these questions about *why,* in my heart I resolved to simply trust. I had to come to the same conclusion Peter did: "Where else could I go, Lord? You have the words of life."(See Johon 6:68.)

After the plane crash I became a lot more dependent on Jesus. I leaned on Him when I did not know what to say to Hannah during the hard times of her recovery. I leaned on Him when I did not know what to say to these families as I tried to bring them some resolution and peace about this tragedy.

I also discovered, all over again, that we're not alone. It seems as though senseless tragedies have happened since the beginning of our Christian faith—from the time when Christians were being lit on fire by Nero; to those who were thrown to the lions in the stadiums; to those who, even today, are martyred for their faith as they go to share the gospel on the mission field, as Jim Elliot did. It seems that, whether heroic or accidental or the result of persecution, good people perish.

God is a mystery. We certainly understand a lot about Him— He sent His Son, Jesus, to show us what He's like, and we have His Word that describes His nature. But we still "see through a glass darkly" (1 Cor. 13:12, KJV). We don't understand everything. God is not a formula. No one person will ever completely figure God out. Despite the fact that circumstances sometimes violate my theology, I trust His nature.

It is so curious to me that in John 6 after Jesus gave this very intense, very difficult message to understand, He did nothing to change the minds of those who were turned off by it. He stopped no one from turning away from Him. Most preachers today (including me) would say, "No, don't leave. Wait! Let me explain this. I can make you understand it. It's not as radical as you think."

But Jesus did not do that. In fact, He turned to the Twelve and asked, "Do you want to leave, too?" (See John 6:67.)

Jesus is the only person I know who ever gave an altar call for people to *leave Him*. Can you picture it? The venue is packed, the invitation is given, and people respond by filing out. As they do, the preacher says, "I see that hand. Just walk out that door."

BELIEVERS *BELIEVE*

After people streamed out of Jesus's meeting and He asked His Twelve whether they were ready to leave Him too, Simon Peter replied, "Lord, to whom shall we go? You have the words of eternal life" (v. 68).

I wonder what was going through Peter's mind as Jesus said these controversial things. I have to believe that Peter was just as confused as anyone else. He had to be thinking, "Eat Your flesh and drink Your blood? What is *that* about?" Yet at the same time Peter's heart had been filled with life from the words of Christ, so his only response was, "Where else can we go? You have the words of life. We have to follow You."

> God is not a formula. No one person will ever completely figure God out. Despite the fact that circumstances sometimes violate my theology, I trust His nature.

Scripture does not elaborate, but it is easy to imagine how Peter would have expressed his confusion and his faith in our modern vernacular: "Jesus, I don't understand this teaching, and I don't really like it. It doesn't make a lot of sense, and it even freaks me out. But what Your words have done inside my heart is so much bigger than the fact that I don't understand this particular teaching. One teaching that I can't grasp is not enough to chase me away from You. You have a hold on my heart. You filled it full of life. How could I leave

You? So I am going to follow You even though I don't understand You at this moment."

I wonder if this was Jesus's point all along—to search out the ones who believed, no matter what. Certainly, the disciples learned more about the blood and the body later, at the Last Supper when Jesus said, "This is My body broken for you. This is the cup of the new covenant in My blood." (See 1 Corinthians 11:24–25.) They got to understand it, because they stuck around long enough to hear more. If the others had stayed, they would have understood it as well.

Jesus is still looking for the kind of commitment that says:

I will follow You even when I don't understand Your words...
Even when I don't understand my circumstances...
Even when everything seems to be falling apart...
Even when nothing really makes sense anymore.

If I hear a sermon or read something in the Bible that I don't understand, or if something happens that doesn't line up with my theology, it doesn't mean I'm going to stop following the Son of God, who gave His life for me. This thing is bigger than my logic, circumstances, or understanding. He has the words of life that have captured my heart.

This is the foundation upon which we build a vibrant relationship with Christ. Even when we don't understand, we follow the rightful owner of our lives And in Him we can develop a strong, resilient faith.

BECOME RESILIENT

- When we don't understand we choose to trust.

- What we believe influences how we perceive things.

- When things don't line up with our theology, we don't stop following Jesus. We trust that we will understand in time, but even if we don't ever understand, we choose to follow and trust.

If you've had a hard time following Jesus because something in your life doesn't make sense or doesn't line up with your theology, I encourage you to choose to trust. Echo the words of Peter, "Where else could I go, Lord? You have the words of life?"

Lord, there are things I don't understand, but I choose to trust You anyway. I repent for allowing my faith to be shaken when circumstances didn't make sense to me. Draw me into a place of revelation. Illuminate Your truth in my heart. I surrender my logic and my understanding. I choose to put my confidence in Your character, knowing You will reveal Your mysteries in Your time. Even when I don't understand, I won't stop following You, because You gave me life. Thank You, Lord for Your faithfulness. This I pray in Jesus's name. Amen.

PART 3

TRAINING TO BE RESILIENT

WITH A SOLID understanding of what resilient faith is, you still have to put in the time to develop it: *you have to train.* As a marathon runner sets her sights on a certain race, you can only finish yours by first preparing for it. You cannot just buy the right shoes and think you are all set. Nor can you strengthen your leg muscles and think you are ready to roll. You must prepare the whole person to run, from head to heart to toe. We need the kind of training that builds endurance. That is the only way we will actually finish our race.

I have to tell you that despite all the training I did, I still experienced pain during my first and second marathons. I had run up to eighteen miles in training without a whole lot of pain. On race day I showed up with fifteen thousand of my closest friends at the Dallas marathon. I was all ready to go at 5:00 a.m. After five miles I was hardly breaking a sweat. Wow! I felt great and went ten miles with no problem. Then on mile eleven I felt pain in my hips. I had *never* felt that pain in my life. When I say pain, I mean pain, pain, pain in every single step.

I thought I would run it off. I went to mile twelve. Still pain in every step. Mile thirteen, fourteen, fifteen—all the way to 26.2 miles. Every single step was painful. Every step was a choice. This is endurance in real life, not theory. My second marathon I hoped for no pain, because I trained much harder. The pain started on mile seventeen. I discovered later that all marathoners experience pain, no matter how many races they have run. So do Olympic athletes and professional athletes. Life is not about avoiding pain but managing it if you want to accomplish something great.

We don't have to wait until challenges come to discover whether or not we will survive. The good news is that the Bible is full of "spiritual exercises" to get us prepared for whatever comes our way. We should never wonder or "hope" we survive. We must prepare and train, so that by God's grace we can join Paul in saying "having done all, we stand" (Eph. 6:13).

Chapter 14

STRENGTH TRAINING VS. ENDURANCE TRAINING

I WAS THE PERSON who hated running. After two miles I would be in so much agony that I'd want to stop. Then my daughters, Hannah and Charity, asked me to run a half marathon with them, and I agreed to do it. I endured hours of agonizing pain, and after it was all over, I decided I would never run again (except to the kitchen to get something out of the refrigerator).

A few years later Charity (my younger daughter) decided to run a full marathon. It inspired me so much that I decided to get back in the game and run a full marathon that was several months away.

Because I had heard about people who actually die while running marathons, I read up on how to train properly. The whole thing scared me a little. It is not that I didn't look forward to dying and being with Jesus someday; I was just not ready to die right away, and especially not after four hours of pain (before the pain, maybe, but not after).

So in desperation I devoured every morsel of information I could find and prepared for the run of my life. One of the terms that kept coming up in the articles I found was *endurance training*. The words always seemed to be italicized by writers who wanted to emphasize the difference between endurance, speed, and strength training. They are all related, but endurance training is different from the other two. To finish a marathon, you have to endure; and to endure, you have to train.

The Bible talks about endurance too. It is essential when running the race called life. Resilient people have *learned* to endure. Yet remarkably there is very little teaching about it. The writer of the Book of Hebrews addressed this important subject. In fact, he made a very strong case for spiritual endurance training. The training he described was all about following Christ's example:

> Therefore, since we are surrounded by such a great cloud of witnesses, let us throw off everything that hinders and the sin that so easily entangles. And let us run with perseverance the race marked out for us, fixing our eyes on Jesus, the pioneer and perfecter of faith. For the joy set before him he endured the cross, scorning its shame, and sat down at the right hand of the throne of God.
>
> —Hebrews 12:1–2

The passage commands us to run the race with endurance. It says we cannot finish the race without it. In other words, *endurance is what makes us resilient.* Paul wrote in Acts 20:24, "My only aim is to finish the race." The apostle was determined to endure. He knew that our Christian life is a race with a finish line we must reach.

So why do we hear so little about endurance? We hear a lot about being strong in the Lord. The tricky thing is that we can be strong physically, but not for very long. Even if we can press iron, we often lack the stamina to stay in the race. When it comes to being resilient, *stamina* is the operative word. We need the ability to bounce-back and sustain our strength. We need to keep going and going like the Energizer Bunny. We need to keep going like Agent 007 in the

> Endurance is what makes us resilient.

Holy Spirit. To finish the race, we have to keep going and going no matter what comes against us.

Successful runners must learn to hang in there. So when I decided to run the marathon, I made it my business to study endurance and develop it in myself. I was struck by the fact that *no one finishes a marathon by accident.* They've trained. They've focused. They've developed. Everyone who crosses the finish line first submits to rigorous training. They push their bodies and focus their minds—and they stick with it!

So many Christians start off with excitement, passion, hope, and zeal. They say: "I hope I stay on fire. I hope I make it to the end. I hope I finish my race. I hope I hear the words 'Well done, My good and faithful servant.'" (See Matt. 25:21.)

That sounds like a lot of hope but not much confidence. People who sign up for marathons don't hope to finish. They are determined to finish. They put their minds to doing whatever is necessary to say, "I *will* run the course and finish it." They train. They prepare themselves, physically and otherwise. They figure out what it will take for them to cross the finish line.

So must we. It turns out that there are a lot of parallels between training for a marathon and training to finish our spiritual race. Yet we are not always as serious about our training as marathon runners are. We need to be. And training to *endure* should top our list.

In the next several chapters I will review what I have learned about training to endure, focusing on four critical areas. As you read about these areas, I encourage you to develop your own spiritual training plan so you will build your endurance and finish the race.

BECOME RESILIENT

- No one finishes a marathon by accident. Everyone who crosses the finish line first submits to rigorous training. They prepare their bodies to endure to the end.

- Likewise, resilient people *learn* to endure. They train diligently to finish the spiritual race we are in as Christians.

It is imperative, not optional, if you intend to finish your race—you must prepare.

Lord, I determine that I will finish the race set before me, and I will finish strong. As the writer of Hebrews said, let me run with perseverance the race marked out for me, fixing my eyes on You, the author and perfecter of my faith. Give me the stamina and diligence to commit to the rigors of training so that I will endure to the end for Your glory, in Jesus's name. Amen.

Real-Life Resilient: Umar Mulinde

On Christmas Eve 2011 Ugandan Bishop Umar Mulinde was attacked by acid-throwing Islamic extremists. Mulinde's terrible injuries required numerous surgeries. Fortunately doctors in Israel were able to save the man's sight and hearing.

Even so Mulinde has been in constant pain every day since the attack. "I have undergone pains that I had never imagined in life, and even if I try to explain it, I feel that it's so hard for me to satisfy another person to really understand it all," he said. "But in all, I am glad to see that I am managing to overcome the trauma with courage to endure suffering."[1]

Chapter 15

BUILDING SPIRITUAL MUSCLE

ESILIENCE DOESN'T HAPPEN by accident, just as no one finishes a marathon by accident. We have to prepare. We all have a race to run and we have to prepare to finish it no matter what comes our way.

When I began training for my marathon, I learned a number of things one must do in order to finish the race. Now, please know, I was not committed to winning the marathon; I just wanted to finish it. That was my part—to finish. I think it's important for us to remember that we're not called to win the race; we're called to finish it. Paul did not claim to win his race. He just said, "I have fought the good fight, I have finished the race, I have kept the faith" (2 Tim. 4:7). That is our assignment: to cross the finish line.

The first thing I learned in my endurance training was that to persevere and finish the race, I had to train my muscles to endure. Once I started endurance training, I realized the condition of my muscles could make or break me. To persevere, I had to get my muscles in shape. If I did not, I risked pulling them in the heat of the race. If that were to happen, I could forget about running; I would barely be able to walk. The idea of limping through the race didn't appeal to me, so I decided to train my muscles properly to avoid severely injuring myself.

Part of muscle training is stretching. Runners have to do extensive stretching before and after each run. Skipping this step can cause serious injury. The parallels in the Christian life are obvious.

We need to stretch our spiritual muscles, and life often stretches them for us! Think about all the stretching that occurs: our patience is stretched; our kindness is stretched; our love is stretched to the limit. All of it prepares us to finish our race.

Besides stretching, runners have to roll out their muscles. The process is fairly painful; it involves a Styrofoam roller that gives athletes an intense form of self-massage. Perhaps you've had a massage that was so deep it was actually painful. That is what runners are encouraged to do. Rolling out your muscles creates deep pressure that hurts, but it helps.

Runners also are encouraged to take ice baths after a long run to help repair their muscles. Ice baths cause the capillaries to constrict and gets the toxins out. The result is the next day the pain in your legs isn't as intense.

Whether running a physical or spiritual race, training is a process. I learned that after a very long run, I needed *not* to run the next day. I paced myself, doing long runs once a week. I started off with eight miles and increased the length incrementally. All the while, I worked on conditioning so my muscles could handle longer and longer distances.

Being Strong Isn't Everything

As I mentioned in the previous chapter, we talk a lot about being strong in the Lord when what we really need is to focus on enduring to the end. Even if our muscles are really strong, they can fail in a long race if they are not trained to endure. It's not just about how solid your legs are but whether they are trained to keep going until the race is finished.

We are naturally good at sprinting. Think about what happens each January: every gym on the planet recruits new members by offering discounts. Owners know that people make New Year's resolutions to lose weight and improve fitness. They flock to the gym, saying, "This is the year I will get in shape!"

Gym owners know that if they get these people committed to annual memberships, the automatic monthly bank deductions will roll in. Although new signups will pay for the year's membership, few will use their contracts to their full advantage. Some will quit after a couple of months. Others will show up, but do more watching than working.

Imagine if someone went to the gym and just watched people work out and then blamed the gym for his poor results: "That gym membership is not helping me a bit! I get there, people are sweating and working hard, and I'm watching them and trying to get into it, but when I leave I'm not any stronger at all. It's a stupid gym! I'm not going back!" It seems obvious: it doesn't matter whether you *join* the gym; you have to *use* it. Unless you lift the weights yourself and train your muscles yourself, you will not get stronger or better.

> Whether running a physical or spiritual race, training is a process.

This is exactly what too many people do on Sunday mornings and Wednesday nights. They go to church and watch other people work out. They watch their pastor, their youth pastor, the worship leader work out, pumping iron as it were, talking about their faith and what God has been speaking to them, but they don't do any work of their own. They may shout amen, but after two or three or four months, or even two or three or four years at the same church, they'll complain that they're not growing. They'll say, "I don't know about that church. It just doesn't help me."

It doesn't do you much good to just watch other people work out their spiritual muscles. You must work out your own. Think about it like this: if you get serious about fitness and hire a personal trainer, you do not pay someone to work out for you. You are paying a professional to get in the gym with you and push you. Your trainer might scream, yell, motivate, and encourage you, but he or she cannot exercise for you. You have to do your own push-ups, pull-ups, and bench presses.

It would be ludicrous to suppose that you could become fit by watching someone else do the work. Yet many Christians think, "If my pastor or my parents or somebody else were stronger in the Lord, I would be stronger." Isn't that equally ludicrous? No one can do your spiritual workout for you—you have to do your own.

WORKING THE DISCIPLINES

If you want your spiritual muscles to get strong and become resilient, you have to be the one who works out. So the question is: How do you work your spiritual muscles? *Is it possible to do physical things that achieve spiritual results?* That is the question of the ages, and it turns out that it's actually possible! In fact, from the very beginning our spiritual fathers taught us spiritual disciplines. These activities engage body and mind for the sake of strengthening their spiritual muscles.

A word of caution: all too often spiritual disciplines are turned into to-do lists designed to make God love us more. The concept could not be further from the truth. The disciplines we are about to explore are designed to get our minds and hearts into a certain disposition so we can hear from God. We are not trying to earn anything. We are simply trying to get our muscles in shape so we can receive from the Lord. Then, as we receive, we become stronger and full of life.

Some of these disciplines will be more familiar to you than others. As you read, think about how they can help you to build spiritual muscle:

- *The discipline of prayer:* This is a regular, consecrated quiet time focused on engaging with God. It is an honest conversation with Him, not just a time to ask Him for things or to dream about all the things you want to see happen. That being said, it is a perfectly good time to express your concerns to the Father who loves you.

- *The discipline of Bible reading:* This is the daily reading of Scripture. Whether you read one chapter per day or ten, whether you read the entire Bible in a year or two or more, reading it is a discipline. That means you do it when you feel like it *and* when you don't.

- *The discipline of silence:* Many early church fathers practiced silence. Some do the same today, whether for a day, a week, or some other increment of time. It is a powerful practice, because our world is full of noise. Decide to be silent, and find out what the Lord might speak to you.

- *The discipline of service:* This is about serving others instead of self. Whatever you do—scrubbing, building, doctoring, or comforting—you will sense God pouring His life into you as you pour your life out to others.

- *The discipline of observing the Sabbath:* Observance of the Sabbath is one of the Ten Commandments. The point is to consistently set the day aside because it is the Lord's Day. It is for fellowship, for being filled with Him, and for drawing closer to Him.

- *The discipline of fasting:* Fasting is abstinence from physical food, so you can focus on spiritual food. It is a time for devouring Scripture. Notice that when the Pharisees turned fasting into a ritual, Jesus rebuked them; but He still encouraged His disciples to fast. Fasting has many benefits. Over the years I have fasted in a variety of ways. I might abstain for three days at a time or for ten or more. Often, I take only water, but I have done broader liquid fasts for up to forty days. Either way, I don't just fast from food—*I feast on Him.* (You can fast from things you love: sugar, media, Twitter, or Instagram. This type of fasting demonstrates self-control.)

- *The discipline of solitude:* This means spending time away from people so you can be with God only. It is another way of drawing closer to Him and moving more intentionally toward Him.

- *The discipline of reflection:* This is about taking time and finding a place to think. Sneak away from your fast-paced world on a regular basis, and simply reflect. You will be surprised by what happens.

- *The discipline of Scripture memorization:* Memorizing passages of Scripture is a powerful way to renew your mind. You might memorize a chapter or even a book of the Bible. I can almost hear you say, "I can't even memorize the things I need to know for work or school." Don't let your past experiences stop you. You can do this! As you heard me say in an earlier chapter: it is time to memorize Jesus's lyrics.

- *The discipline of worship:* This means spending time in God's presence. It does not necessarily include music. Worship is when you honor God for who He is and humble yourself before Him, submitting yourself anew to His lordship. When we worship we are able to draw near to God and commune with Him.

Our spiritual fathers taught us how to build our spiritual muscles. When you are disciplined, you don't *hope* to meet a challenge or finish a race; you *prepare* to do so. When I started that first full marathon, I knew I was going to finish because I had trained to endure; I worked on getting my muscles in shape. There was no reason to worry about the outcome, because I had prepared myself to cross the finish line.

Spiritually speaking, too many Christians kind of hope and pray that they will make it to the end of their lives still loving Jesus. You don't have to do that! Prepare now with your spiritual disciplines. Remember that you are not trying to earn something from God by practicing the spiritual disciplines. We practice them because we were changed in the deepest way by Jesus. We practice spiritual disciplines to get ourselves into a position to hear from God, and as a result, our spiritual muscles are strengthened.

BECOME RESILIENT

- We all have a race to run, and we have to prepare to finish it no matter what comes our way.

- We will never become fit by watching others work out. No one can do our spiritual workout for us. We have to do it on our own.

- Spiritual disciplines engage the mind and body to help strengthen our spiritual muscles. They are not meant to become a legalistic to-do list. They help get our hearts in a disposition to hear from God and receive from Him.

You don't have to merely hope you reach the end of your race. You can prepare to do so. At the end of this chapter is a chart you can use to track how often you are training your spiritual muscles by practicing the spiritual disciplines. Now, ask the Lord to help you commit to incorporating the spiritual disciplines discussed in this chapter into each and every day.

> *Lord, I want to become strong in You. I want to build my spiritual muscles so I can endure to the end. I commit now to spending time with You each day practicing spiritual disciplines. Let this become second nature so I don't spend a day without building myself up through prayer, Bible reading, solitude, reflection, and the like. I want to hear Your voice and receive all You have for me so I can make it to the end strong and resilient, in Jesus's name. Amen.*

SPIRITUAL DISCIPLINES LOG

Spiritual Discipline	Sunday	Monday	Tuesday	Wednesday	Thursday	Friday	Saturday
Prayer							
Bible reading							
Service							
Observing the Sabbath							
Fasting							
Solitude							
Reflection							
Scripture memorization							
Other							

Chapter 16

CARDIO CONDITIONING

T O ENDURE A marathon and to be resilient in the race of life, you must make sure your heart is in great shape. I have learned a lot about what happens to your heart and to your lungs as you get in good shape. It turns out that the average body has about a million miles of arteries and capillaries. Capillaries are the tiniest blood vessels. They help carry oxygen to your extremities to nourish and strengthen the muscles.

As you exert yourself, more capillaries are created. This raises your oxygen capacity so that more oxygen is carried throughout the body, including to your lungs. If you run a ten-minute mile tomorrow, your heart rate will rise and your breathing will become heavy. But if you run a ten-minute mile every day for a week, your breathing will gradually improve as your body grows more capillaries. With a more efficient circulatory system, you don't need to breathe as heavily to keep your muscles nourished. At the same time, the more panting you do, the more waste you unload. All of this increases endurance. As you exercise your cardiovascular system, you create the capacity for resilience.

The process of becoming spiritually resilient is similar. In each case, your heart needs to be in great shape.

WHAT DOES THIS HAVE TO DO WITH OUR SPIRITUAL LIVES?

Spiritually speaking, the Holy Spirit is our oxygen. This is the presence of God. John 20:22 says that the resurrected Jesus breathed on His disciples and they received the Holy Spirit. To maintain the level of our spiritual oxygen, we must pace ourselves and keep our hearts pure.

Even if we attend the most on-fire church in the world, we still live in an impure world. We "inhale" the world's toxins every day through media, music, the Internet, and advertising. Toxins are everywhere. Like smog in a polluted city, they tend to leave their residue on us.

Jesus said, "Blessed are the pure in heart, for they will see God" (Matt. 5:8). Jesus was explaining how important it is to keep your heart in good shape and to eliminate the toxins that work to corrode it. No matter how pure your heart is today, toxins will find their way in tomorrow. Don't become like so many who have gone to church or to youth group for years, only to discover that they no longer sense God's presence. They say, "I can't feel Him. I can't hear what He's saying. What's wrong?"

Jesus said that if you are pure in heart you *will* see God. You will sense Him; you will hear and understand His ways and His heart—if you keep your heart in good shape.

SO WHAT DO WE DO?

If you want to be in good physical shape, you need a cardio workout at least several times a week. To be in good spiritual shape, you need your spiritual cardio workout every day or two. What I mean is this: you need to examine your heart and look for toxins to unload.

We all need this! So we can pray as David did: "Search me, O God...and see if there is any wicked way in me" (Ps. 139:23–25, NKJV). When we pray this way, we say, "God, the residue of the world is on me. I want to exhale; I want to repent. Please purify my heart."

That is what repentance is—getting the garbage out of our lives. Even when we follow Christ, the residue of the world tries to land on us. Every day we need to shower ourselves under the grace of God. Just as we must inhale oxygen to live, we must have the capacity to "inhale" the Lord's presence. As we exhale the world and its attitudes, we increase our capacity for Him. When we exhale the world and repent, saying, "God, cleanse my heart," God breathes His life in us, filling our hearts to capacity.

With our hearts functioning this way, we sense Him, we see Him, and we walk with Him. This is why we must know the condition of our hearts. We need to ask ourselves whether we have emptied out our cardio waste. Jesus said if you have a pure heart you will be blessed and you will perceive God (Matt. 5:8). So if it has been hard to connect with God, we know there is more exhaling to do—it's time to get in a cardio workout.

> Even when we follow Christ, the residue of the world tries to land on us. Every day we need to shower ourselves under the grace of God.

BECOME RESILIENT

- To endure a marathon and to be resilient in life, you must make sure your heart is in great shape.

- Spiritual "toxins" are all around us. We "inhale" them through media, music, the Internet, and advertising, and they leave their residue on us.

- When we do spiritual cardio, we examine our hearts for toxins and then unload them. By doing this regularly, we will keep our hearts in good shape.

- When we repent and ask God to cleanse our hearts, He empties us of the world's toxins and breathes His life in us. This allows us to sense God's presence.

If you've been struggling to sense God's presence, why not stop now and pray this prayer?

Father, if there is any wicked way in me, give me a pure heart. Get the toxins out of my system so I can see You, hear You, and sense Your presence all day long! In Jesus's name. Amen.

CARDIO WORKOUT LOG

Did you spend time with the Lord today, emptying out the cardio waste and purifying your heart so God can breathe His life into your heart? You can pray as David did by simply saying: "Search me, O God and see if there is any wicked way in me. The residue of the world is on me. I want to exhale; I want to repent. Please purify my heart." We need to go before the Lord regularly to purify our hearts. Use the following chart to track how often you are doing your spiritual cardio.

HAVE YOU DONE YOUR CARDIO WORKOUT TODAY?

MONTH: _____							
	Sunday	Monday	Tuesday	Wednesday	Thursday	Friday	Saturday
Week 1							
Week 2							
Week 3							
Week 4							
Week 5							

Chapter 17

SPIRITUAL NUTRITION

MY WIFE IS a health-food queen. I'm a junk-food king. If it tastes like cardboard, Katie loves it. She has been trying to get me to eat more healthily for years. Nothing worked. But when I started studying in earnest about how to train for a marathon so I wouldn't die trying to finish, I learned a lot about nutrition and how it enables runners to finish the race.

Marathon runners live with an ever-present fear of "hitting the wall." This tends to happen at around mile twenty or twenty-two of the race, when the runner's body is so depleted of energy that he or she collapses. Some runners feel a lot of physical pain. Some feel really tired, and others just give up.

When you hit the wall it is possible to push through to finish the race, but it is excruciating on many levels. When I first learned about it, I assumed it was inevitable that every runner would hit the wall at some point. Then in my preparation for the marathon, I read something that forever changed my thinking. It said: "*Only ignorant and uninformed people hit the wall.*"

Whoa! I could hardly believe what I'd read. If only ignorant and uninformed people hit the wall, then I knew I could prevent myself from doing it. And if it was possible to keep from hitting the wall, then I decided I was *not* going to be ignorant and I was *not* going to be uninformed. Once again I devoured every piece of information I could find to learn how to avoid hitting the wall.

I thought about this in terms of Christianity too. Spiritually speaking, people hit the wall all the time. We all know someone about whom we say, "So-and-so used to be so on fire. What happened? I haven't seen him in church in months, or even years." Or, "I heard she started hanging out with this crowd. I heard she's mad at the church and doesn't want anything more to do with God."

When our Christian friends hit the wall, we wonder, "What happened to them? Why did they throw in the towel? What caused them to collapse?" Instead of living in fear that the same thing might happen to us, we can make sure it doesn't. One of the best ways to avoid hitting the wall is to get excellent spiritual nutrition. The right "food" will keep us resilient to the very end.

It works a lot like physical nutrition does. I learned from my research that the right physical food gives you the right kind of energy. You have probably heard about good carbs and bad carbs. Your body converts everything you eat, whether carbs or protein, into energy, and that energy helps you keep going. The problem is that some things are harder to convert than others. Certain foods take a lot longer to break down. Some start out fatty or convert to fat when you eat them. Some convert to instant energy; some don't.

In running you need a nutritional strategy, because what you eat needs to keep giving you energy. Without a strategy you *will* run out of energy and hit the wall. In training for the marathon you not only need to eat the right carbs, but you also need to consume the right number of carbs. Before your big run, you can "carb up" by eating lots of pasta in the days leading up to the race. Then during the run, you have to carry the right nutrition with you so you can keep yourself fueled. If you eat bad carbs, they will actually send you on a low. So even though they taste good, they will suck the energy out of you.

PLAN YOUR INTAKE

Let's talk about your spiritual nutrition. Where is your energy coming from? Are you living on fresh manna, or are you still munching on something you learned a year or two ago? Are you totally reliant on what your pastor preaches, or do you forage for your own food between services?

What kind of "carbs" are you consuming? Are you concentrating on "bad carbs," as it were—media, movies, news, and video games? If that's all you're putting inside all the time, it's no wonder you don't have any spiritual energy. If you stuff yourself with the wrong things, you won't have room for what's good for you.

Think back to a great Thanksgiving meal that you looked forward to. Perhaps your mother was preparing the feast—turkey and all the fixings. You decided to starve yourself all day so you'd have room for this great dinner, but by early afternoon you were so hungry, you ate some chips to tide you over. Unfortunately one chip turned into a whole bag. By the time dinner was served, you were no longer hungry.

> What kind of "carbs" are you consuming? If you stuff yourself with the wrong things, you won't have room for what's good for you.

You were so bloated with junk your appetite was spoiled. Now you have a fantastic meal in front of you, complete with homemade dessert, and you're no longer interested in eating it.

I wonder if that is what happens to many Christians on Sunday mornings or on other mornings when they sit down for their quiet time with God. He has prepared a beautiful meal for them to consume, but they are so filled with the world's messages that their spiritual bellies are bloated and their appetites are spoiled. They are so stuffed, the meal God is fixing does not even look appealing.

Could it be that we need to cut back on the "junk food" of the world so that we are hungry for the nourishment we really need—the feasts God offers us each and every day? That's something to think about.

We need to ask ourselves, "How much spiritual food am I eating? Do I eat only at church?" What would you think if someone said, "I know you need food to survive, so I'm going to feed you on Sundays and Wednesdays." We'd think that person was out of his mind! Nobody would agree to that. If we wouldn't try to survive on eating physical food only on Sundays and Wednesdays at church, why would we do that with our spiritual nourishment?

If you do realize your need for physical food, the next question you must ask yourself is, What kind of spiritual food am I eating? Are you eating spiritual junk food? Are you only listening to messages that tickle your ears or make you laugh? I am not saying that humor is ungodly. What I am saying is that we cannot listen only to messages that make us feel good. Spiritual junk food is like physical junk food. If you eat chips and candy bars all the time, you're going to get fat and bloated, and you won't be prepared to endure to the end.

The writer of Hebrews warned about this. In essence he said: "By now, you should be able to eat meat, but I have to give you milk. You should be eating red meat, but I can only give you the milk of the Word." (See Hebrews 5:12–14.)

My challenge is this: plan a solid spiritual diet for yourself. Plan your menu by listing all seven days of the week and the things you will read and listen to on each. Include books, podcasts, and other sources that you know will challenge you. Allow them to provoke you to repentance where it is needed. Be thankful when they reveal areas in which you are weak and need to become strong. For instance, if you find it difficult to be generous, seek out teachings and mentorship in the area of generosity and giving.

It is like our moms told us: we have to eat our vegetables, in this case our spiritual vegetables. We need to absorb the right nutrients and address any deficiencies. If we are serious about finishing the race and not hitting the wall, it is imperative that we do so.

BECOME RESILIENT

- Marathon runners can become so depleted of energy that they "hit the wall" and collapse. This can happen to us spiritually as well.

- One of the best ways to avoid hitting the wall is to get excellent spiritual nutrition.

- Just as in the natural, if you fill up on spiritual junk food (by listening, for example, only to messages that make you feel good), you won't have room for those things that are spiritually nutritious. As a result, you will get fat and bloated and won't be able to endure to the end.

- Plan a solid spiritual diet for yourself filled with resources that will challenge and provoke you, and strengthen areas of weakness.

Don't waste any time. Use the chart at the end of this chapter to develop your spiritual nutrition plan for the week. Let's pray for the Lord to guide you as you create this plan.

Lord, I don't want to be like the people the writer of Hebrews talked about, who are still drinking the milk of Your Word. I want to be mature, so I can handle meat. Show me areas of weakness in my life and direct me to resources that will help me address them. I want to be challenged so I can be changed. Help me to become strong so I can endure, in Jesus's name. Amen.

SPIRITUAL NUTRITION LOG

Spiritual Nutrition	Bible Study	Other reading	Ministry podcast	Topics I want to explore and grow in strength
Sunday				
Monday				
Tuesday				
Wednesday				
Thursday				
Friday				
Saturday				

Chapter 18

FOCUS ON THE FINISH LINE

To be resilient, you must also train your mind on the finish line. One of the things I learned while preparing to run a marathon is that you can have your muscles trained well, you can have great nutrition, your can be disciplined in your cardio, but if you do not determine that you *will* finish, you most likely won't. Even if there's no physical reason for you not to cross the finish line, if you don't see yourself completing the race *before* you run it, you just won't finish.

Your state of mind must be deliberate. We don't become resilient and stand strong in the midst of crisis by accident. There are many times during a race when you don't feel like running at all. All you want to do is quit. Physically you are spent, done, empty, but you *focus on finishing* the race.

I wonder if this is why Paul talked in Philippians 3:13–14 about pressing toward the goal. Paul said things like this over and over again. In Colossians 3:2 he wrote: "Set your minds on things above, not on earthly things." With all the distractions pulling at our attention from every direction, it is easy to lose our focus. For example, the average American teenager sees sixty thousand hours of movies and television by the time he graduates high school. By contrast, that same teen spends eleven thousand hours in the classroom and only eight hundred hours in church.[1]

Whether you are a teen or an adult, you are swamped by distractions. With so many options screaming for your attention, it is easy to wander off course. But you don't have to. You can and must run your own race. No one can run it for you. Only you can train yourself to do this. Hebrews 12:2 says you can do it by considering the example of Jesus, "who for the joy that was set before Him endured the cross, despising the shame" (NKJV).

Notice what Jesus did: He focused on His goal—the joy before Him. We must do the same. We won't reach the finish line by accident. We will finish because we prepared to be resilient. In large part that means avoiding chronic busyness and anything that might poison our minds.

> Even if there's no physical reason for you not to cross the finish line, if you don't see yourself completing the race *before* you run it, you just won't finish.

We wouldn't eat poison or do something intentional that would kill our body. So why would we poison our mind with things that directly oppose Scripture?

A few days after the plane crash I attended the funeral for Austin Anderson. It was moving to see two thousand people gather in his small town to honor his life, including a number of his fellow Marines. I met with Austin's family, encouraged them, and listened to their stories. It was difficult for me to get through the funeral without losing it, partly because he and Hannah were friends and he had recently joined the staff at Teen Mania. But it was also because I knew he likely played a role in helping Hannah survive the crash.

I was given the opportunity to speak, and part of what I shared with the attendees is the fact that en route to the event, where they were going to worship the Lord with twenty-five hundred other young people, four of those on board the plane instead encountered the ultimate worship service in heaven. They were on their way to learn how to help a whole generation meet Jesus face-to-face, and then in a moment they met Jesus face-to-face.

Austin, Luke, Stephen, and Garrett were determined and focused, consumed with God's call on their lives to make a difference in this world. Rather than focus on starting big, money-making careers after graduating with business degrees, Austin and Stephen instead decided to become part of Teen Mania and do everything they could to rescue this generation. In the middle of that focused mission God had for them, they lost their lives. What better way to go? They died in pursuit of a mission, and in doing so, joined the ranks of people such as John the Baptist, who was jailed for sharing the gospel and killed because of the ridiculous whim of a king, and Jim Elliot and Nate Saint, who lost their lives while in pursuit of their mission to reach the Auca Indians.

What better way to meet Jesus face-to-face—when you're all-consumed and focused on what He has called you to do, throwing yourself into and spreading His message, abandoning every other possible treasure and honor that the world might offer; then in the next moment, there you are with Him. The way those four young men went to heaven is the way I want to go: focused on the call until the very end.

In our fast-based culture it's so easy to be consumed by things that are small and unimportant. Put aside time-wasters and things that oppose God. Learn what your priorities are and eliminate activities that have no real or lasting importance.

A poem reportedly written the night Japanese forces burned Shanghai during World War II reflects the folly of chasing trivial pursuits:

> Tonight Shanghai is burning
> And we are dying too
> What bomb more surely mortal
> Than death inside of you?
>
> For some men die by shrapnel,
> And some go down in flames

But most men perish inch by inch,
In play at little games[2]

This could not be truer than of this generation, which has games at their fingertips all the time. We *must* stay focused on the finish line!

PLAN TO FINISH STRONG

Part 3 of this book discusses spiritual things in practical ways. My encouragement, even before you read another page, is to apply what you learn. Invest time in your spiritual workout plan. Decide now what you will do about the spiritual disciplines mentioned earlier. Put together a calendar. Pencil in the things you will do each day, each month, and every quarter to position yourself to hear from God.

Come up with your own cardio plan. What will you do on a regular basis to clean up your heart? By all means plan to attend an Acquire the Fire event or a revival at your church, but don't wait for special occasions to ask the Lord, "Is there any wicked way in me?" Have a plan to keep your heart clean and free from the world's debris every day.

Give thought to your spiritual nutrition. Feed yourself seven days a week on Scripture. Listen to teaching CDs and podcasts. Weed out the media sources that distract you from becoming resilient; find the materials that build your endurance and strengthen your spiritual muscles.

Each and every day make sure your mind is set on finishing the race. See yourself crossing that finish line. Imagine hearing Jesus say, "Well done, good and faithful servant!" (Matt. 25:21).

If you cannot picture this in your mind, it probably won't become your reality. You have to train to be resilient. That is how you make sure you are prepared to be resilient when times are hard and the world seems to be crashing in around you. Resilience does not just happen. You become resilient because, by the grace of God, you *prepared* to finish the race.

BECOME RESILIENT

- If you don't prepare to finish the race, *you won't.*

- Focus on the finish line by avoiding distractions. Put aside time-wasters and pursuits that draw you away from God.

- Each day imagine yourself finishing the race. See yourself crossing the finish line and hearing Jesus say, "Well done, good and faithful servant!"

Resilience doesn't happen by accident. We must be intentional. Let's pray for the grace to be deliberate about keeping our eye on the finish line.

Put your spiritual workout plan together right now and plan now to start your workout tomorrow!

> *Lord, I know there are times when I won't feel like pressing on. There will be times when I want to quit. Help me to keep my eyes on the finish line. Let me focus on the goal so that I don't give up but endure to the end, in Jesus's name. Amen.*

Chapter 19

ROT-PROOF YOUR ROOTS

I N SO MANY different places throughout the New Testament, metaphors are used to compare spiritual growth and plant life. Here is a great example from John's Gospel:

> I am the true vine, and my Father is the vinedresser. Every branch of mine that does not bear fruit he takes away, and every branch that does bear fruit he prunes, that it may bear more fruit. Already you are clean because of the word that I have spoken to you. Abide in me, and I in you. As the branch cannot bear fruit by itself, unless it abides in the vine, neither can you, unless you abide in me. I am the vine; you are the branches. Whoever abides in me and I in him, he it is that bears much fruit, for apart from me you can do nothing. If anyone does not abide in me he is thrown away like a branch and withers; and the branches are gathered, thrown into the fire, and burned. If you abide in me, and my words abide in you, ask whatever you wish, and it will be done for you. By this my Father is glorified, that you bear much fruit and so prove to be my disciples.
>
> —JOHN 15:1–8, ESV

In talking about vines, branches, and pruning, Jesus gives us a lesson on spiritual health and the importance of staying connected to Him. It's amazing how detrimental eliminating these metaphors can be to our own spiritual growth.

Psalm 1:3 says that we can be like trees planted by living water.

If you asked most people, "In your walk of faith, do you want to be as strong as that tree?" they would say, "Yes." The tree is a picture of resilience. However, it's not uncommon even for massive trees to be blown over in big storms. In fact, on our campus in East Texas, we've had giant oaks literally uproot and fall over while other trees stood strong right beside them.

A good question for us to ask ourselves is, "What will I look like after the storm?" Storms will come and when they come, will we be uprooted and snapped in two? Or have we learned how to stand strong? Do we try to "get strong" only when the wind comes and the storm begins? Or are we training for strength over time?

Why is it that some trees fall and others don't? Why is it that some followers of Christ succumb to the storm while others don't? The answers to these questions are key to understanding resilience.

WHAT KIND OF TREE ARE YOU?

According to Psalm 1, we are to be like trees planted by rivers of living water. Let's examine several different types of trees, assess their strengths and weaknesses, and see how they relate to different "types" of Christians.

Softwood trees

These are pine trees or balsas. They are generally large trees. They grow fast, but they have no real strength. You can't build much with them. Some Christians are like softwood. They've been around for a long time, but they're soft inside; they have no strength. You can't build anything with them.

Junk trees

These are hackberry trees and other species that are actually overgrown weeds. They grow the quickest, but they have the shortest lifespan. The only things they are really good for are shade and appearance. That's what some Christians are like. They are only good for show. Their loud mouths are full of Christian platitudes, but they don't get deep roots and eventually die.

Thorny trees

These have sticky, nasty leaves. Some of them are sweetgums. Some have thorns that stick and jab when you run through the woods. Others have spiky seed pods that fall and feel like glass when you step on them. Thorny trees have giant aberrations that can hurt you. Some Christians are like thorny trees. They have giant aberrations in their character that hurt other people. Their words and actions cause wounds. The fruit of their lives is the pain they cause for others. We should ask ourselves whether we have any giant aberrations that are hurting people.

Baby trees

We all know that when we first plant trees, it's smart to put two or three poles around them with guide wires to hold them up. That way, when storms come the trees won't get blown over. Some people think they are going the extra mile by leaving the poles and guide wires up for two to four years instead of just one. They believe they are helping their trees, but they are actually hurting them. After the supports are finally removed, trees that had them too long often get snapped in two or uprooted when the first storm comes.

There is something about the resistance of the wind and the storms that makes trees strong. The wise cultivator takes the guide wires off after a year. Then as smaller storms come, the trees grow and build resistance in their root systems so they're not easily blown over. They also grow resilience in their trunks so they are not easily snapped. Many Christians are like baby trees. They are glad to have guide wires, but they've been "in the greenhouse" too long. They are afraid of storms. They try to duck around them. They've never learned to resist the winds of temptation when the enemy comes. They've never had to develop a backbone. They are on "spiritual crutches" for the rest of their lives. It's time for all of us to grow up and remove our guide wires. It's time to let our root systems grow deep so that we can withstand the storms of life.

Dead branch trees

Some trees are full of dead branches. Soon after we moved to Texas, I woke up to find my car's back window bashed in by a big, dead branch that had fallen from high up in a tree. Jesus mentioned that unfruitful branches need to be trimmed back (John 15:2), but many people carry dead branches around with them. There are areas where they're not bearing fruit or ugly areas and habits that are hurting other people. These fruitless deeds of the flesh are causing destruction to other people's lives. We need to look at ourselves and ask: "Are there any dead branches that I need to break off of my life?" Do you have living branches that need pruning? Jesus said that even fruitful plants are trimmed in order to be more fruitful. It's true in almost every plant: bushes, rosebushes, and fruit trees. When you trim them, they sprout more. They bloom more. They bear more fruit. Just letting them grow whichever way they want is not helpful. Pruning them and guiding their growth is. This is what Jesus was referring to in John 15. God wants to prune your fruitful areas so they can be even more fruitful.

ROOT ROT

Trees need a good root system in order to grow and remain strong. It's imperative that cultivators pay close attention to the root system. In Matthew 13:5–6, Jesus talked about plantings that lack depth of soil and proper roots. He was talking about the importance of Christians having deep roots so they are not easily distracted by the cares of this world.

Let's take a look at issues that hinder the growth of healthy root systems.

Root problems

Because many trees lack the right soil environment, they develop what's called "root run." There may be insufficient nutrition in the soil or too much iron. Sometimes the roots just don't grow down as deeply as they need to. They may have been overwatered, saturating the roots and causing them to rot. Maybe the roots never penetrated the ground and just continued surfacing.

I've seen amazing pictures of trees literally growing into the sides of mountains and into rocks in the Grand Canyon and other places. What an amazing thing to see roots penetrating rock to get to the nutrition they need! The question is: Are your roots deep in the rock of Christ? Do you have the right conditions in the soil around you so your root system can thrive, and so you can thrive as a strong tree in this world?

Galatians 5:22–23 talks about the fruit of the Spirit: love, joy, peace, patience, kindness, goodness, faithfulness, gentleness, and self-control. Please note that fruit trees don't *try* to grow fruit. They just grow fruit because they are fruit trees. If they are planted in good soil, the fruit naturally grows. Too many of us Christians are forcing ourselves to be patient and kind instead of thinking deeply about where our roots are and what kind of nutrition we are soaking up. We need to question what we are listening to and what we are ingesting. These are the things that affect our health, but they happen beneath the surface and are not obvious to other people. So are you creating conditions for spiritual growth in your life? What are you listening to? What are you watching? Who are you hanging out with? How are you feeding your soul? What books

> Are your roots deep in the rock of Christ? Do you have the right conditions in the soil around you so your root system can thrive, and so you can thrive as a strong tree in this world?

are you reading? How are you spending your time? When you tend to these things properly, you become a tree planted by the living water.

Pests

Enemies and intruders can eat their way into root systems. One of the biggest enemies of large trees is one of the smallest creatures: the black carpenter ant. These ants can grow up to half an inch long. I've seen an army of them in my own yard. They're not called carpenter ants because they have hammers and nails; they're called carpenter ants because they actually eat the insides of trees. They burrow their way under the ground, into the root system, and up the center core of the tree. I've seen trees actually die as a result of infestation. When diseased trees are cut down, you can see six-inch wide tunnels that have been eaten away by hundreds of thousands of ants. They have literally *eaten away the core of the tree.*

The question is: Do you have any black ants eating away at your core? Are there things that you tolerated because you didn't think they were a big deal until they brought all their friends in to eat away at your strength?

These "pests" come in all shapes and sizes. Some are like pine beetles; they can kill a whole forest of pine trees. The problem is that the affected trees look strong on the outside until the very end. Then a storm comes and they snap in an instant. Some die more gradually. Some Christians are gradually dying too—dying because of what they have allowed to live inside of them. Just as a small ant can kill a big tree, the smallest of sins or habits can kill you. Even though you are getting stronger in the Lord, even though your roots are strong, you still have to be on the lookout for the pests that the enemy of your soul sends to try to destroy you. Bugs, sins, and deceptions are trying to lure you away. Storms will come, but what happens to you depends on what you are doing right now when there is no storm. Ask yourself: Why do some fall and others stand strong? Neither outcome is an accident. Those who stand are determined to get their roots down deep. By the grace of God they find His strength to fend off the enemies who seek to eat away at their core.

You can be the Psalm 1 tree that is firmly planted by living water. You were created to be a strong tree with a healthy root system. You can withstand every storm and turn away every foe. You are resilient.

BECOME RESILIENT

- You can withstand every storm if you stay connected to Jesus, the vine. Allow yourself to be pruned, and you will bear much fruit.

- Find out what kind of tree you are and determine to remain planted by the living water.

- Don't strive to grow fruit; allow yourself to be fruitful *because you were designed to bear fruit in Him.*

Be committed to having a healthy root system. Refuse to tolerate conditions and pests that weaken you over time. Develop habits that build spiritual strength.

> *Lord, I am sorry for not paying attention to where my roots are. I know that if they have the right conditions I will produce fruit for You. Today, Lord, Help me prevent root rot by putting the right ingredients in my heart. In Jesus's name. Amen.*

PART 4
THE FURY OF THE RESILIENT

W<small>E ARE IN</small> this fallen world, but we are not of it. To run the race to the end we have to consciously reject the world's tendencies. By God's grace we must resist the temptation to compromise or quit. We choose not to be counted among the deserters who look over the fence for greener grass.

The resilient are a fierce bunch because they follow the Lion of the tribe of Judah. They are relentless, not because they are high and mighty, but because He is almighty. They learn the difference between the roar of heaven and the roar of the impostor, and they finish their work while it is light. Individually, and as a people, they leave a legacy—*of resilience.*

Chapter 20

A TALE OF TWO DESERTERS

RESILIENT PEOPLE ARE constant. They do not fly the coop at the first sign of trouble, or wander from the fold every time something rubs them the wrong way. Resilient people know how to endure over the long haul, because they have trained themselves to do so.

In this chapter I want to share two powerful stories of those who were not resilient. These stories illustrate the deserting heart. One story is two thousand years old. The other began in the twentieth century. Despite the millennia separating them, the stories are remarkably alike.

AN ANCIENT DESERTER

In Luke chapter 15 Jesus tells the story of a famous deserter known as the prodigal son:

> There was a man who had two sons. The younger one said to his father, "Father, give me my share of the estate." So he divided his property between them. Not long after that, the younger son got together all he had, set off for a distant country and there squandered his wealth in wild living.
> —LUKE 15:11–13

The prodigal son deserted because of unresolved issues in his heart. He knew he would receive an inheritance when his father died, but he was not willing to wait that long. He was impatient, not only to get the cash, but also to spend it.

> After he had spent everything, there was a severe famine in that whole country, and he began to be in need. So he went and hired himself out to a citizen of that country, who sent him to his fields to feed pigs. He longed to fill his stomach with the pods that the pigs were eating, but no one gave him anything. When he came to his senses, he said, "How many of my father's hired servants have food to spare, and here I am starving to death! I will set out and go back to my father and say to him: Father, I have sinned against heaven and against you. I am no longer worthy to be called your son; make me like one of your hired servants."
>
> —LUKE 15:14–19

This young man was unprepared to make it at home and equally unable to make it on his own. He planned on living it up (which he did), but he soon found himself in worse shape than pigs in a pen.

His life was an undeniable mess, but the mess got his attention. Filthy and starving, he humbled himself and returned home.

> So he got up and went to his father. But while he was still a long way off, his father saw him and was filled with compassion for him; he ran to his son, threw his arms around him and kissed him. The son said to him, "Father, I have sinned against heaven and against you. I am no longer worthy to be called your son." But the father said to his servants, "Quick! Bring the best robe and put it on him. Put a ring on his finger and sandals on his feet. Bring the fattened calf and kill it. Let's have a feast and celebrate. For this son of mine was dead and is alive again; he was lost and is found." So they began to celebrate.
>
> —LUKE 15:20–24

The prodigal son made the best possible choice in a very diffi-cult situation. He admitted his failures and acknowledged his need. He humbled himself before his father, whom he had earlier treated with such arrogance. Despite the damage the son had caused, the father welcomed him home with open arms.

When we lack resilience and even when we fail miserably, we have a Father who loves us and longs to restore us. If we are humble, desertion is not the end.

A Modern Deserter

The prodigal son's story reminds me of another deserter I read about not long ago. In 1965 a twenty-four-year old Army sergeant named Charles Robert Jenkins was stationed near the demilitarized zone between North and South Korea. Jenkins had served in the military for some time, but the dangers of patrolling the Korean border started to become more than he felt he could take. When he learned he would soon ship out to Vietnam, he felt he had to do something.[1]

One night after drinking ten cans of beer, Sergeant Jenkins decided to desert the US military. While out on a late-night patrol, he decided to make his move. He told the troops with him to go on ahead. As they did, he slipped away and passed into North Korean territory.

Sergeant Jenkins was immediately taken captive. He thought in the back of his mind that the North Koreans would trade him to Russia, which would then deport him to the United States in some kind of Cold War swap. That never happened. Instead, Jenkins remained a prisoner of the North Koreans for forty years.[2]

Jenkins endured harsh physical treatment by his North Korean monitors and was forced to become well versed in his captors' com-munist propaganda. For seven years straight he had to study the writings of North Korea's dictator for eight hours a day, a task made more difficult by the fact that it was written in a language he didn't understand. He never had enough food, and in North Korea's frigid temperatures, he never had enough heat. He eventually married a Japanese woman who had been abducted by the North Koreans. She bore him two daughters[3] whom he believed would be used as spies.[4]

Through a long series of unexpected events and negotiations, Jenkins eventually had the opportunity to come home to the United States. In September 2004, after being allowed to go to Japan to be treated for an illness, he turned himself in at the American military base there. By the time of his surrender he had suffered many ordeals and paid many high costs for his decisions as a young man. His desertion had not worked out as he had planned. The damage he did in 1965 could not be undone. Things had gone too far and there was no easy way out. Sergeant Jenkins, *the deserter,* would have to face military justice.

THE HIGH COST OF DESERTION

Too many Christians are "deserting" their faith because they haven't found the backbone to be resilient. Let's see what we can learn from the prodigal son and Sergeant Jenkins that will keep us from doing the same.

Impact on others

Both the prodigal and Sergeant Jenkins created hardship for themselves and for others. The prodigal squandered a fortune, suffered humiliation, and created a rift in his family (see Luke 15:25–32). Before his desertion, Charles Robert Jenkins had served long enough and with enough distinction to lead US reconnaissance missions.[5] He wasn't a new recruit when he decided to desert. He had been elevated to the status of a sergeant and had soldiers under his influence and control. They looked to him for leadership and safety. Instead, he abandoned them.

Many times when people desert the faith, they think, "It's only about me and my faith. My decisions won't hurt anybody." They don't think about the people around them who are watching them and being influenced by their decisions. They don't think of the destructive impact they may have on someone else's faith.

Have you ever known someone who had been following Christ for years then for some reason disappeared from the faith? Paul mentioned someone like this in one of his letters to his protégé, Timothy: "Demas, because he loved this world, has deserted me and has gone to Thessalonica" (2 Tim. 4:10). Demas's decision no doubt affected others. The event was significant enough for Paul to mention it.

We must check ourselves by asking, "What foundation have I built my faith upon? Is it my parents' Christianity, or do I have a real connection with God that is my own? Is my foundation as solid as I think it is, or have I lost perspective? Am I just going through the motions because of what my family has always done, or is there a genuine love for Jesus burning inside me?"

"Greener grass" syndrome

Both the prodigal son and Sergeant Jenkins thought the grass was greener on the other side of the fence. For the prodigal, freedom and cold cash seemed inviting. Jenkins seemed to think even being in jail in the United States would be better than serving in the military. He thought, "Anything has got to be better than what I am going through right now. All I really need is to get to the other side."

The grass on the other side always looks greener, until we get there. That is Satan's trick. He lures us into sin by convincing us that God is trying to keep good things from us. This is what he did in the Garden of Eden. Centuries later, he tried tempting Jesus:

> The devil took him [Jesus] to a very high mountain and showed him all the kingdoms of the world and their splendor. "All this I will give you," he said, "if you will bow down and worship me."
> —MATTHEW 4:8–9

Deal-making is one of Satan's most productive methods. He knows how to make himself and his offers attractive, especially to those who are sitting on the fence or looking for a way out. Paul warned about Satan's ability to deceive, saying that "Satan himself masquerades as an angel of light" (2 Cor. 11:14).

The problem is this: *those* (including those in the military) *who have deserting hearts are already preoccupied with a longing for the other side.* They're thinking and dreaming all the time about jumping the fence.

Even when the prodigal son lived in his father's household, he dreamed about the other side. This is how many who call themselves Christians are. They go to church. They may even read their Bibles and participate in Christian activities. But they're *longing for the other side.* They're wishing they could attend that party, wishing they could get drunk, wishing they could see that movie, wishing they could be in that relationship they know isn't good for them. They yearn for what's "out there" and act as if they're enslaved to the faith, as though they were horses with bits in their mouths, forced to do the right thing. All the while they're thinking it would be better if they could get to the other side.

When the prodigal son had it good, he longed to leave. I think the tragedy is that he wanted his father's inheritance without having a real relationship with his father. That's what too many so-called Christians want. They want love, forgiveness, and eternal life, but they don't want a relationship with God. As a result, they dream about the other side and believe that God is holding something back from them.

Charles Jenkins's heart left long before he physically abandoned his post. The prodigal son's heart broke from his father long before he asked for his share of the inheritance. Neither man was resilient in the face of temptation.

Some people wonder why they are not resilient when life hits them hard. In part it is because they do not guard their hearts as Scripture says believers must (Prov. 4:23). We *need* to guard our hearts from wandering and longing for the things of the world. And if we find ourselves longing, we need to repent and say, "God, give me new longings that are pure and holy."

If we long for the other side, we will inevitably go there. If our hearts leave, it is just a matter of time until the rest of us leaves to find the elusive "greener pastures."

Regrets

Sergeant Jenkins "realized almost immediately he made a mistake."[6] When he was arrested, he was overcome by remorse. The illusion that had deceived his heart—about a better life, more freedom, and getting out of the military—came crashing down around him.

The same thing happened to the prodigal son. He spent all of his fortune, and had nothing to show for it—*nothing*. Having money and so-called freedom did not make his life better. Things got so bad that he found himself longing to eat slop with the pigs.

Scripture says the prodigal "came to himself" (Luke 15:17, NKJV). The New International Version says, "he came to his senses." Finally the blinders came off and he realized, "Man, I blew it!"

> If we long for the other side, we will inevitably go there. If our hearts leave, it is just a matter of time until the rest of us leaves to find the elusive "greener pastures."

This is the point at which most deserters have a chance to turn around, as the prodigal son did. Unfortunately turning around is not always instantaneous. Once Sergeant Jenkins realized that he'd made the worst decision of his life, there was no easy way out. It would take him almost forty years to return to US custody.

Life gets worse

Charles Jenkins thought it was bad being arrested, but his situation continued to get worse. He was kept in prison, forced to recite communist mantras in Korean, even though he didn't know that language. If he made a mistake he would be beaten. If he failed to memorize the specified amount, he would be beaten. In addition to worrying about his own well-being in North Korea, he also feared for his wife and daughters. He suspected the marriage had been arranged to produce more American-looking children who could be turned into spies.[7] During the almost four decades in North Korea, Jenkins found no peace.

Sin always takes its toll. Scripture says in Galatians 6:8: "Whoever sows to please their flesh, from the flesh will reap destruction." No matter how promising the other side looks, or how the enemy dresses it up, life always gets worse for deserters. It might not happen immediately, but it does happen.

Sergeant Jenkins tried to make a life for himself in prison. He was married to a woman who had been abducted from her native Japan, and they had two children. Though their marriage was arrange by the North Korean government, it seems they tried to make a pseudo life.

This happens so often. When we desert, we rationalize and try making the best of the hellhole we've found ourselves in. Sin becomes a substitute for real joy. We end up making ourselves a life in the pigpen and say, "Oh, the slop's not so bad!"

The whole time, we are in slavery.

Most people without Jesus routinely live this way. They talk about all the great things going on in their lives. They boast about their cars, houses, jobs, families, and all the adventures and excitement they enjoy. They try to make it sound good, but it is *all they have.*

It is a little easier to understand how people without Jesus live this way. It is more unsettling when people who call themselves Christians create pseudo lives in "foreign" lands. These are people who "prayed a prayer" but are living without the blessing of God on their lives. They have filled their minds with excuses about why it is OK to do whatever they want. They defy the evidence in Scripture that it is *not* what God wants for them. They continue to pretend that life in the pig pen is OK.

More false promises

When you take the enemy's bait and agree to become a deserter, he continues to deceive. Once he has you where he wants you, he will do almost anything to keep you there. When international petitioning created a pathway for Sergeant Jenkins and his family to leave North Korea, he promised Pyongyang that he would return. They in turn promised him a list of perks that far exceeded anything he had ever enjoyed in North Korea.[8]

They knew he would never want to return, so they kept making him promise after promise. This is exactly what the enemy does, and too often we believe the lie. We'll repent and get out of the prison we made for ourselves, then, just as a dog returns to its vomit (Prov. 26:11), we'll start to think, "It wasn't that bad. It worked out OK." We forget the horror and the brokenness we found ourselves in, and open ourselves to more of it. Too often, we find ourselves going back again and again to the thing that destroyed us in the first place. This ought not to be.

Real-Life Resilient: North Korean Christians Return Home

The prospects for Christians living in North Korea are anything but good. If their faith is discovered, they are sentenced to life in one of the nation's prison camps (among the most brutal in the world) or executed outright. There is no doubt that for North Korean Christians, life looks greener on the other side of the demilitarized zone.

Amazingly, some Christians who escaped the tyrannical nation have felt a strong calling from God to return to North Korea, to spread the gospel message. They will risk everything to share Jesus with the people of North Korea.

The following is part of a prayer a believer about to return to North Korea prayed:

"Please provide me with Your power and wisdom, so that I can preach Your love to the people in my country and help them to live according to Your words. Please help us to accept Your words and guide our lives without any fear or worries.... I will return back to North Korea without any fear and worry. It is because God is with me."[9]

THERE IS ALWAYS HOPE

On September 11, 2004, Sergeant Jenkins turned himself in to the United States Army at Camp Zama in Japan. He knew he faced consequences for his desertion, but he no longer saw the grass on the North Korean side as being greener. "'I have made my peace with the U.S. Army,' Jenkins said after his release, 'and they have treated me very fairly.'"[10]

Jenkins was not concerned about his own needs any longer. When asked about his daughters, he replied: "I just spent 25 days in jail. I haven't really gotten a chance to talk to them that much yet. But I think they will be all right." He starts to sob. "I made a big mistake of my life, but getting my daughters out of there, that was one right thing I did."[11]

Jenkins knew that, technically speaking, he could have been sentenced to death. He was not, and the sentence he received was minimal. He did not object to incarceration. He accepted the punishment as a fair price for the peace of finally making right choices. His attitude was similar to that of the prodigal son who said, "I'm no longer worthy to be called your son, I'd just like to be a slave in your house if I could."

This is the attitude we should have when we come back from our deserting.

BECOME RESILIENT

Let's cap the subject of desertion with some key points that can help us identify and correct any tendencies to chase whatever we think we see on the other side of the fence:

- *The heart of a deserter wants only benefits, with no relationship.* The prodigal son wanted his dad's stuff, not a relationship with his dad. He was attracted to the blessings, but turned off to responsibility. This is a worldly approach to life, and the world continually taunts us with it. In order not to be deceived by it, we have to examine our hearts and expose any deserting tendencies. We need to recognize that the moment we begin to long for the other side—the enemy will work to draw us there.

- *The heart of a deserter inevitably produces the life of a deserter.* Some people who have already deserted in their hearts are looking for any excuse to leave their faith. If one prayer is not answered or one Christian lets them down, they are gone. If you find yourself longing for the "greener" side, repent—*immediately*. Even as you long to satisfy yourself with those deceptive pleasures, ask God to give you a heart that craves what is pure and holy. If you arrest your deserting heart, you won't follow it to the other side. (Remember that believers typically have hearts that long for God. It is the flesh that longs for evil; that is what God must cleanse us from.)

- *A returning deserter must have a heart of genuine repentance,* saying, "The ramifications do not matter. It doesn't matter what price I have to pay, I must come back." The question is, "When?" If we discover we have a deserting heart, or if we are already living a full-on deserted lifestyle, how long will we linger in the pigpen before we make up our minds to leave it? Will it take us forty years, the way it did Sergeant Jenkins? Or will it start now? Are we so afraid of the repercussions that await us that we'd rather stay in the slop? Or do we believe that renewing our relationship with the Father is the most important and worthy choice we can make?

None of us is entirely innocent in this area. Every one of us eventually experiences a situation in which deserting seems like the easiest solution. Thank God we have a High Priest who will graciously rescue us if we ask Him to. Let the following prayer open the door to your heart, and His help:

Lord, forgive me for sometimes longing for the other side. Forgive me for being deceived by the enemy and for thinking that life without You (and outside of Your will) is a more attractive option than serving You. Lord, guard my wandering heart that it might be solely Yours. Forgive my deserting lifestyle. I repent! I come running back to You. May my heart always be true, in Jesus's name. Amen.

Chapter 21

THE ROAR OF A LION

S EVERAL YEARS AGO my family and I took a mission trip to Africa. We spent time in Kenya in Maasai territory, where many great safaris are held. Of the forty-two tribes in Kenya the Maasai have managed to hold on to their culture. Their distinctive dress and their ability as hunter-warriors are legendary. They are a nomadic people who live in constant danger of being attacked by wild beasts. Maasai warriors are trained to fight these animals, including the most feared—the lion.

Today some Maasai people are coming to Christ! Pastor David, our tour guide in Kenya, is a former Maasai warrior. What I learned from him about the tribe's warrior training was both shocking and illuminating.

When Maasai boys are young, they are trained to resist pain. Their baby teeth are intentionally cut out by adults who tell them they cannot cry or whine over the discomfort. If they do, the children will be beaten. When they get older, some of their adult teeth are cut out. Again, they must not cry or flinch, or they'll be beaten.

The young boys also have their ears pierced with red-hot rods. If they cry or scream, they will be beaten. When other skin is ritually burned with red-hot metal, the same rules apply. No flinching or crying are allowed. When the young men are thirteen or fourteen years of age, they are circumcised in front of the tribe. As always, if they scream or complain they will be subject to severe beating.

All of these rituals are designed to prepare young warriors to endure pain, struggle, and challenges. The ultimate goal is to equip each one to prevail over the feared lion. They must be ready to endure whatever is necessary to protect the village from the king of the beasts.

One of the final steps in becoming a Maasai warrior comes when the young men and tribal elders leave the tribe for a three-month period in the woods. There, they eat cows and herbs and are taught to kill lions with nothing more than their bare hands, a stick, a spear, and a sword.

You might wonder, as we did, "How in the world can you kill a lion with a stick, a spear, and a sword?" This was the question we begged of Pastor David. He explained that as part of the three-month training, each potential warrior is required to face a lion and either kill or maim it, or be killed or be maimed. Every Maasai warrior has done this.

The young trainees must listen at night to locate and surround a lion in the jungle. One trainee is selected to face down the beast. The young warrior-in-training typically holds his spear in his left hand. The stick is about a foot long and has a point one each end. The beast has learned to fear the spear, so he lunges at the hand with the spear, which is typically the left. In that moment, the fighter must switch hands. Now the stick is in his left hand and the spear is in his right.

As the lion moves to clamp down on the left hand, the boy jams the stick in the lion's mouth. Now the lion's mouth is lodged open with a sharp point on the top and the bottom. Meanwhile the young warrior-in-training uses his right hand to spears the lion in the neck or heart. At that point, the lion will hesitate and fall back for a minute. Then the would-be warrior grabs his sword and slices the animal's loins until he bleeds out.

To the Western mind, the ritual seems brutal. For the Maasai it is essential to survival. It is an amazing feat of hand-eye coordination.

Once he has defeated the lion, the young man has reached the status of Maasai warrior and is allowed to go back to the village and choose a girl there as his wife!

What courage. What strength. What *resilience.*

FIGHTING THE IMPOSTOR LION

This is the warrior spirit I believe the Lord wants to develop in every follower of Christ. Scripture tells us that Jesus is "the Lion of the tribe of Judah" (Rev. 5:5). He is tough. He is fierce. And He is looking for us to grow a backbone and hate the devil.

Scripture says, "Your enemy the devil prowls around like a roaring lion looking for someone to devour" (1 Pet. 5:8). The devil impersonates Christ by putting on a lion persona. Unless we are trained to have a warrior backbone like the Lion of the tribe of Judah, we could be easily intimidated by the impostor. We might hear his roar and forget whose we are.

We are called to confront this "lion," but how? And how do we defeat him? How do we prepare ourselves to face the lions of temptation and intimidation? The only way is to be trained by the Lion of the tribe of Judah, Jesus. We have to learn to take pain, to grow strong, to be strategic, and *think.* We must prepare to protect ourselves and our families from this world. We must take back everything the devil has stolen.

> Unless we are trained to have a warrior backbone like the Lion of the tribe of Judah, we could be easily intimidated by the impostor.

We cannot do this by accident. We must be trained. We must develop a spine, hate sin, love what is true, and resist the devil so he will flee (James 4:7).

It is interesting to note that in the Maasai culture, every boy is *required* to be a warrior. It is not voluntary. It's mandatory. Somehow in our Christian faith we think it's optional to learn to resist the enemy and be strong in the Lord. Many of us believe that only a few elite Christians are required to do the fighting and be resilient. The reality is that we all must be trained to face down the impostor lion that stalks and tries to devour all of us. Unless we learn to fight, we *will* be devoured.

THE LION AND THE LAMB

Jesus is both the Lion of the tribe of Judah and the "Lamb of God who takes away the sin of the world!" (John 1:29, NKJV). How is it possible to be both a lion and a lamb? Lambs are tenderhearted and humble in demeanor. Lions are nothing like lambs.

Jesus was moved with compassion to see His people scattered like sheep without a shepherd (Matt. 9:36). He is gentle, humble in heart, and cares about us. Jesus also roared like a lion. You can see the fierceness of His convictions in a number of situations. He accused the Jews of making His Father's house a den of thieves. (See John 2:16; Matthew 21:13.) He also told the scribes and Pharisees, "You are like whitewashed tombs…full of dead men's bones" (Matt. 23:27, NKJV). Jesus did not hide His contempt for the two-faced hypocrisy of religious-looking people.

Scripture says other things about Jesus. It says He "endured the cross, despising the shame" (Heb. 12:2, NKJV). On our behalf, He endured whipping, mockery, and pain, and revealed His quiet dignity in the process. Think about it: Jesus hung on the cross for six hours, but barely spoke for a total of sixty seconds during that span of time.

Consider the quiet dignity of the statements Jesus made as He suffered:

1. "Father, forgive them, for they do not know what they do" (Luke 23:34, NKJV).

2. "Truly I tell you, today you will be with me in paradise" (Luke 23:43).

3. "Woman, behold your son!...Behold your mother!" (John 19:26–27, NKJV).

4. "My God, My God, why have You forsaken Me?" (Matt. 27:46, NKJV).

5. "I thirst!" (John 19:28, NKJV).

6. "It is finished" (John 19:30).

7. "Father, into your hands I commit my spirit" (Luke 23:46).

This is how we endure. This is how we are resilient: with quiet dignity and confidence in our God. Scripture says that we have not resisted sin to the point of shedding our blood (Heb. 12:4). We think we are fighting hard against sin, but we have not fought to the death. Scripture tells us to endure as soldiers. Hebrews 12:7 says: "Endure hardship as discipline; God is treating you as his children. For what children are not disciplined by their father?"

When we face challenging situations, we can choose to see them as periods of discipline, our training to be resilient. Note I said discipline, *not* punishment. This discipline is making us better, like the discipline of working out or the discipline of running. It's getting us in shape to endure! Instead of feeling sorry for ourselves and complaining about our pain, we can see that our training is making us better.

Masai warriors-in-training understand and endure strong discipline. It prepares them to face down lions in hand-to-hand combat! As we face challenging times in our lives, we are doing the same: we are learning to defeat the one who stalks us, the one trying to destroy us.

Jesus told us to endure to the end (Matt. 24:13, NKJV). He knew we were going to need a backbone. He knew we would need courage. He understood that we would suffer hardships, false prophets, temptations, and possible torture. There would be challenges in our marriages, and we would have to learn to work things out in our other relationships. We would face difficulties with our children and with life in general.

Jesus knows what is ahead. He says, "Listen, you *must* have a backbone if you're going to follow Me. You have to be resilient. You need courage. Forget about your feeble needs. Learn from Me. Be strong in Me."

Being resilient is not about how great we are, but how mighty He is. I love what Paul says in 2 Corinthians 4:7–11:

> We have this treasure in jars of clay to show that this all-surpassing power is from God and not from us. We are hard pressed on every side, but not crushed; perplexed, but not in despair; persecuted, but not abandoned; struck down, but not destroyed. We always carry around in our body the death of Jesus, so that the life of Jesus may also be revealed in our body. For we who are alive are always being given over to death for Jesus' sake, so that his life may also be revealed in our mortal body.

Paul said, I'm pressed but I'm not crushed. I'm enduring some tough times, but it has not obliterated me. I've got the fire and the life of God burning inside me!"

THE REALITY OF PAIN

One of the things I learned after my second marathon was the reality of pain. Even though it started several miles into the race, the pain was excruciating through every step. I was hoping to be in such great shape that there would be no pain at all, so I pushed all the harder in my training for marathon number two. Yet in talking with other marathoners who had much more experience than I had, I realized that *every marathon runner endures pain.*

You cannot complete a race without pain. Any professional or Olympic athlete has to deal with it. You can never eliminate pain; you must learn to manage it. You have to figure out how to handle your mind and heart. How will you prepare yourself so that when pain and other challenges come, you can face them down?

Preparing for pain is hard because we've become consumed with avoiding anything and everything that is uncomfortable. We have become pain-avoidance experts. We think that avoiding pain is a sign of strength. The real strength is found in being resilient. That kind of strength is not loud, obnoxious, or arrogant. It is a controlled type of strength, or what Scripture refers to as *meekness.*

Do you remember when a village of Samaritans rejected Jesus's message and His disciples wanted to retaliate? Luke 9:54–56 says:

> When the disciples James and John saw this, they asked, "Lord, do you want us to call fire down from heaven to destroy them?" But Jesus turned and rebuked them. Then he and his disciples went to another village.

Do you remember when Jesus was arrested and His disciple cut off a man's ear? Jesus was not looking for human protection. He asked, "Don't you think I can call a legion of angels right now?" (See Matthew 26:53.) He was saying, "Look, I've got the power, but I'm not exercising it." In John's Gospel, He made it very clear: "No one takes my life; I lay it down. I've got the power to lay it down and to take it up again." (See John 10:17–18.)

Jesus was strong; Jesus had a backbone. He showed us how to be resilient, even when the whole world comes against us.

We need to think about how committed we are to pain avoidance. How have we navigated around painful situations or complained our way through issues that were less than pleasant? As a result, how have we failed to develop the strength those challenging times would have produced in us?

Let's embrace the discipline we need so that when real challenges come along, we are ready to endure. It is time to get into training. We must face the lion that prowls and stalks us so we can represent the Lion of the tribe of Judah and be resilient, until the very end.

BECOME RESILIENT

- The Lord wants us to develop a warrior spirit so we can confront the enemy instead of being intimidated by him.

- Jesus is "the Lion of the tribe of Judah" (Rev. 5:5). He is tough. He is fierce. And He wants us to be the same.

- We can choose to see challenging situations as periods of discipline—our training to be resilient. This discipline is not punishment. It's making us better and getting us in shape to endure!

- Many of us have become experts at avoiding pain, but it's impossible to complete a race without it. Instead of trying to eliminate pain, we must learn to manage it. That way when challenges come, we won't run from them. We will face them down.

The resilient aren't afraid to fight. They don't run from the devil. I encourage you to ask God now to develop within you a warrior's heart.

Lord, create in me the heart of a warrior. Let me not shrink back when the enemy attacks. Let me not fall into the trap of intimidation. Teach me to embrace discipline and manage the pain that is sure to come. I want to represent You well, as a good soldier who is willing to endure hardship. Teach me to walk with quiet dignity and confidence in You, the Lion of the tribe of Judah, in Jesus's name. Amen.

Chapter 22

THE RESILIENT ARE RELENTLESS

T HINK ABOUT THE one thing you desire more than anything in life. You may have wanted it when you were young. Perhaps you could not wait until Christmas to get it. Maybe you saved up for it and finally got it a year later. What other things do you crave? Fame? Money? A boyfriend or girlfriend? A degree? Marriage? More stuff?

Everyone wants something. Jesus addressed our wants and our needs in the Sermon on the Mount:

> Therefore I tell you, do not worry about your life, what you will eat or drink; or about your body, what you will wear. Is not life more than food, and the body more than clothes? Look at the birds of the air; they do not sow or reap or store away in barns, and yet your heavenly Father feeds them. Are you not much more valuable than they? Can any one of you by worrying add a single hour to your life? And why do you worry about clothes? See how the flowers of the field grow. They do not labor or spin. Yet I tell you that not even Solomon in all his splendor was dressed like one of these. If that is how God clothes the grass of the field, which is here today and tomorrow is thrown into the fire, will he not much more clothe you—you of little faith? So do not worry, saying, "What shall we eat?" or "What shall we drink?" or "What shall we wear?" For the pagans run after all these things, and your heavenly Father knows that you need them. But seek first his

kingdom and his righteousness, and all these things will be given to you as well.

—MATTHEW 6:25–33

Jesus was saying, "I don't mind you having stuff, but I want you to seek Me first. I want to be the all-encompassing love of your life."

In this world there is always a carrot dangling ahead of us. It is human nature; we always seem to be chasing something. And once we get it, we want something else. It never ends. We think if we had that car or that house or that job, our lives would be bliss. Yet we are never satisfied. When we get those things we want something else. We cannot wait until next Christmas or our next birthday to get that one thing we have always wanted and even begged to have. Then, two days later we don't remember where we put the thing. It seems we have an insatiable desire to pursue things, and those things leave us empty.

I remember hearing about a man who won hundreds of millions of dollars in the lottery and pledged to give a portion of the winnings to his church. He and his wife did give generously to churches and other causes, but their lives soon fell apart.

The man was constantly being asked for money, for things as trivial as new carpet and entertainment systems. Their true friends seemed to have disappeared. But what was worse was what happened to their family. They had started giving their teenage granddaughter $2,000 a week and bought her several new cars. They started seeing her less and less as she began to hang out with a rough crowd, who introduced her to illegal drugs. She'd be gone for days at a time until finally she left and never came back.

> In this world there is always a carrot dangling ahead of us. It is human nature; we always seem to be chasing something. And once we get it, we want something else.

After a two-week search her body was discovered wrapped in a sheet and dumped behind a van.

I remember seeing this man's tear-filled eyes in a TV news report. He was so broken. The granddaughter he loved so dearly was gone. The things the world says are important only left him empty. The man said, "I wish I'd torn that ticket up."[1] The very thing so many people dream of having—hundreds of millions of dollars—destroyed this man.

PURSUED BY GOD

In Matthew chapter 6 Jesus talked about seeking *first* the kingdom of God. He knew that we humans would always seek *something*. But instead of seeking things we think will make us happy, He told us to seek His kingdom first.

When we anticipate getting the things we have longed for, we experience a kind of euphoria. It is the hope that getting these things will make our lives better. We are tantalized, even intoxicated by the idea. The payoff always seems bigger and better than what we imagine—until we get it. Then there is a letdown. Everything feels good for a moment, but before we know it we're on to the next thing.

The way we pursue things is the way God pursues us. Matthew 13:45–46 describes a passionate pursuit: "The kingdom of heaven is like a merchant looking for fine pearls. When he found one of great value, he went away and sold everything he had and bought it."

The kingdom is like the man who finds the treasure in the field. We are that treasure, and God relentlessly pursues us. In fact, He's pursuing every single human being everywhere in the world. He has pursued us from the very beginning, in the Book of Genesis. He knew Adam and Eve had sinned, but He returned to the Garden of Eden and asked Adam, "Where are you?" (Gen. 3:9). Instead of being angry at Adam, instead of striking him with lightning, God pursued Adam, and cried out, "Where are you?"

God is in hot pursuit of you and of me. He pursues what He values. Because He values you and me, He sent His Son, Jesus, to pursue us. If we really knew how much we were valued, we would never try to earn our value again with how we dress, how much money we make, how good we are at sports, how popular we are, or by puffing ourselves up and bragging about what we can do. If we really knew our value, we wouldn't perform to get other people's approval. We would know that God loves us as we are; His approval would be all we ever needed.

The maker gives value to the things He makes. Just as a manufacturer sets the prices on his goods, God set His price on us. We are His treasure.

You are the treasure He pursues; that is why He sent Christ—*for you.*

Not only is God relentlessly pursuing all people, but He is also pursuing *every part* of each of us. He doesn't want a quick prayer or just sections of our hearts. He wants every piece of every life. For the rest of our lives, He will show us those areas that we have not fully surrendered to Him. He persists so that we *can* surrender and make more room in ourselves for Him.

Imagine your life is like a house. You invite Jesus into your house, but without realizing it, you treat Him like the uninvited vacuum cleaner salesman who just rang your doorbell and is really pushy. You don't want to let the salesman in at all, but if you are feeling really generous, you might let him into the foyer. You give him a few moments to give his spiel, and you send him away.

Is that what you do when friends come to your house? No! You give your friends whatever they want whenever they want it. You empty out your fridge for them. You hang out with them, whether it is convenient or not. You make them feel welcome. You want them to feel at home.

If only we did that with Jesus! Instead, we act as if He is trying to sell us something. If we let Him in at all, we confine Him to the stuffy part of our house, the part that is prim and proper. That is what we do at church, so we do it in the living room. We sit up straight and mind our manners.

That is not what Jesus is pursuing at all. He wants to come in and be familiar with us. He wants to know our hearts, our homes, and our lives. He is not looking just to visit. He wants us to give Him the keys. After all, He is in charge. He wants to go through the whole house and clean it up.

So what do so many of us do? We tell Jesus, "You can come into my life, but don't go into that closet over there. It's too private. I'll talk to You about it later."

There are some areas of our lives that we're ashamed of. We have suffered pain because of things that have happened to us, or things that we have done to ourselves or others. But He is not ashamed. He wants to come into those areas as well. He relentlessly pursues every part of us. He is not a stuffy Sunday-morning God. He is looking for us to open up the whole place. He wants to come in, rearrange the furniture, knock down some walls, redesign the whole house if He wants to so it's to His satisfaction. He is not content with a quick visit in the foyer.

How should we respond? We need to stop pursuing whatever it is we are pursuing besides Him. Anything that serves as a substitute for Him must go. Anything that we run to in order to run from Him, we have to let it go. We must simply stop and pursue Him only.

BECOME PURSUIT-MINDED

How do we become pursuit-minded?

1. Be aware that God is pursuing you, and let Him catch you!

Let Him find you and let Him catch you. You don't have to be perfect for Him to be pleased with you. You are the gold He seeks, just as you are. And He is the greatest "prize" you can possibly desire. The euphoria that you seek in life can only be found in Him.

2. Surrender all of your house to Him.

Let Him have your whole heart, your whole life—even the parts you have been hiding from Him. If you have told Him: "No, You can't go into my friendship closet; I keep my friends to myself. I don't want You telling me what to do in the media area of my life. I'll make those decisions. And when it comes to who I'm dating, that area of my life is all mine," it is time to surrender. Just say, "OK. You're chasing after every part of me, so I'm going to surrender every part of me."

It takes humility to do this. It takes a heart of surrender.

3. We must change our pursuits and the direction of our pursuits.

That is what Jesus was talking about when He said, "Seek first the kingdom of God" (Matt. 6:33). There is only one way that I know this can happen: it is by daily asking for a miracle in your heart and crying out for this miracle every day. Pray, "God, give me a heart that pursues You relentlessly...that seeks You relentlessly."

As A. W. Tozer wrote: "God discovers Himself to [us]."[2] God shows Himself to those who are hungry for Him. Many passages of Scripture describe the hunger that draws this response from God. Psalms 42:1 says: "As the deer pants for streams of water, so my soul pants for you, my God." Matthew 6:21 says: "Where your treasure is, there your heart will be also." Matthew 13:44 says: "The kingdom of heaven is like treasure hidden in a field....In his joy [a man] went and sold all that he had and bought that field."

This is what God is looking for: people who will turn and relentlessly pursue Him.

If you are one who will do that, He will fill you with life, with joy, and with strength. Nehemiah 8:10 says, "The joy of the LORD is your strength." That is the joy that makes us *resilient.*

BECOME RESILIENT

The resilient are the relentless. They don't try to build themselves a backbone so they can brag in their own strength. They are the ones who surrender to Him. They let Him capture them. They surrender every part of their "house"—their hearts, their lives, their *everything* to Him.

They choose each day to say, "I'm going to pursue You, Lord, with all that I am and have. By reading, praying, listening, I will fill myself with Your truth. Then I know You will fill me with Yourself. Your joy will give me the strength to be resilient."

None of us is capable of the perfect pursuit of God. We get distracted. Things happen that get us off track. But God is both gracious and merciful. All we need to do is to be honest about the struggle and ask for His help.

Whenever you get tangled up in pursuing something besides Him, just pray:

> *Lord, Jesus, I release all of the things I have pursued outside of You today. Whatever things are of this world, I choose to stop chasing them. Instead, I focus on You. I desire to seek You first. I surrender all the parts of my heart and life that I have kept locked away. I open the "closets" that I have not allowed You to enter. Today, Lord, I ask You for a miracle, a change in my heart. I ask You for the yearning to relentlessly pursue You, because in that, I am completely filled. In Jesus's name. Amen.*

Conclusion

THIS IS OUR HERITAGE, OUR TRIBE

Aafter the shock of the plane crash wore off, reality hit Katie and me. Hannah was in the hospital in Kansas City for the first four weeks to get skin grafts and daily "scrubbing" of all the new skin. This is an excruciating process necessary so infection does not set in. I spent every night with her in her hospital room. When we moved her to Dallas on a medevac flight, I flew with her and stayed with her in the rehab hospital almost every night.

After months of struggle and excruciating pain, Hannah began to make real progress physically. When she was finally ready to come home to complete her recovery, we had no idea how much the work was just beginning. Hannah could barely walk and was on a lot of medicine for pain. She was in constant pain and grief for months. The painful memories of the event would trigger symptoms of PTSD, the same kind that a soldier coming back from the battlefield might experience after seeing his friends perish in front of him.

Katie was really the hero in this story as she waited on Hannah, serving her meals in her bedroom, cleaning up for her, and arranging all the physical therapy sessions. For month after month it seemed that, although she was making physical progress, Hannah's heart and emotions where overwhelmed with grief. As we prayed daily for her and had a number of spiritual leaders come to spend time with her (including Erwin McManus and his daughter, and Dave

Roever and his wife), nothing seemed to assuage her pain, which increased ours. It was a long period of enduring in our faith and trusting in the Lord. Finally after being home for six months, some wise leaders began to help Hannah walk through the grief and begin her journey to wholeness. We could see the hand of God dramatically changing her outlook on life. She is still on her journey of recovery, but well on her way. For the months (that seemed like years) we had to have total trust that God would carry us and her though this and bring understanding at some point. That still has not come. But still, we trust.

PAYING THE PRICE

Throughout these chapters you have read the stories of true disciples from around the world who have agreed to pay whatever price is necessary to follow Christ. As we have searched through Scripture, we have seen that this is what Jesus has always desired. It is the reason He was never too quick to take people when they said, "I'll follow You, Lord!" Instead, He asked them to really think about the commitment they claimed to make. He made them count the cost. "Do you have enough money to build the tower?" He asked, "Do you have enough soldiers to win the war?" (See Luke 14:28–33.)

From the very beginning, these were the kind of followers Jesus wanted. Truly, they are the only followers He is worthy of. He gave His whole life for us. He is looking for the same kind of devotion He showed. He is our example.

Throughout the history of Christianity, we have seen this kind of devotion. The apostles lived for Christ and (except for John) they died as martyrs. Countless disciples were thrown in jail, whipped, or devoured by lions before tens of thousands of spectators. Many were burned alive, serving as human torches at wicked Nero's garden parties. These relentless believers refused to recant, even under threat of death. This is the kind of courage, the kind of backbone believers have had since the beginning of the church.

We were born for this, and our movement, our tribe, was born out of this. In story after story, the evil one tried to crush the church by killing her martyrs. But those who gave their lives for Christ caused more people to believe! Secular onlookers wondered, "Who are these people who would give their lives and endure such torture and suffering for what they believe? I have never met anyone like them before. Maybe I should think about what they believe."

Think about it: if others had not endured, we would never have known about Christ. Those with steel spines throughout the ages passed the faith down to the next generation, and the one after that. Without their stand, the faith would have been stamped out. The only reason we know about grace and forgiveness, the only reason we know what it means to have a new heart, is because of those who were resilient in their day.

Only one question remains: What will future generations say about us? Will they say: "They were faithful. They passed the faith on. When they could have been lulled to sleep by commercialism, capitalism, and pleasure, they endured. They prepared themselves to be resilient, so that when challenges came, they were ready."

It is the resilient who will carry on this legacy. It is the resilient who show God's grace in action. God has always had a remnant that is resilient. He will have one in this generation. The question we each have to ask is, "Will I be a part of it?" It is the resilient who fall so in love in Christ that they cannot be controlled or stopped. It is the resilient like Shadrach, Meshach, and Abednego who have determined how they will live, regardless of the circumstances they must endure.

Consider places in our world today such as Iraq, Iran, and China. Believers in these lands know that in choosing to follow Christ, they will probably go to jail, be kicked out of their homes, be threatened with murder, and maybe even killed. They know it when they decide; but they choose anyway.

If you knew for a certainty that would happen to you when you chose Christ, would you have chosen to follow Him?

Let that question sink in.

Millions of brave men and women around the world know what to expect when they choose Christ. Therefore, they count the cost beforehand. They come to Him knowing what they are getting themselves into. So when persecution comes, they are prepared. They are ready for the consequences.

The price is high, but not too high. Remember that Jesus is the greatest treasure of all. There is no one like Him. He paid the highest possible price for us. As A. W. Tozer wrote: "We owe Him every honor that it is in our power to give Him."[1]

Let us be among the resilient. Let it be because we are in love with Christ and prepared to face even the toughest challenges by God's grace, and with His joy.

Let it be said that we endured...that we were *resilient*.

BECOMING *RESILIENT* STUDY GUIDE

*R*ESILIENT. THAT IS what we are called to be. We will not get there without training, and some *un-training*. We need a little of both to uproot the misconceptions and resistances that hold us back. If we are to establish a faith that sustains us through thick and thin, we must decide to "go there" *no matter what.*

This study guide is designed to help you navigate the road to resiliency. Use it on your own or in a group. Let it bare your heart to the God who loves you and to your own understanding. Process your experiences and thought patterns; let the material draw from you the resiliency that will stand up to surprises and setbacks, whatever circumstances you might face.

These pages will guide you through an eight-week journey. Invest yourself in the transparency and revelation they provoke. Let the questions rewire your assumptions. Allow the Scriptures to strengthen your heart. Watch and pray as the applications convert information to transformation.

And remember: *you were born to be resilient!*

WEEK 1

W E LIVE IN a feel-good world in which we mistake our emotions for the "real us." Too often, instead of focusing on doing the right thing, we cave in to the soul's demands for what makes us feel good. Then, when trials come, we are caught short, believing that "bad things" should not happen to us, because we are Christ's. If this is the "gospel" we believe, is it also the one we share with others? Let's find out!

Read the introduction and chapters 1 and 2 of *Resilient*.

Read Philippians 4:13, Matthew 16:24, and Matthew 24:13.

REWIRED FOR RESILIENCE

Think about a moment when you received unthinkable news. What was your first reaction? How did the news challenge your beliefs?

_____

_____

When you don't understand what is happening or why it is happening, which trusted truths help to sustain you, and how?

_____

_____

Has an unexpected event or situation left you feeling simultaneously thankful and angry? What other conflicting emotions have you experienced? What is the current status of this conflict?

_____

_____

How has our feel-good culture impacted your faith? Are you ever tempted to "go with the cultural flow"? What do you fear might happen if you "swim against the current"?

_____

_____

Describe the world's view of being true to oneself. How does it compare or contrast with godly authenticity? How does knowing the difference clarify your choices in life?

_____

_____

When you first came to faith in Christ, which "plan" did you sign up for? In what ways did the plan prove to be more dangerous, fantastic, or unpredictable than you expected?

_____

_____

How can we present the gospel in a way that better prepares others for the Christian reality? How has the gospel presentation you first heard supported your walk? How has it fostered disillusionment?

_____

_____

RESILIENT IN THE WORD

What does resilience look like in your current circumstances? How do Philippians 4:13, Matthew 16:24, and Matthew 24:13 support your explanation? What other Scripture passages come to mind?

_____

_____

THE ROAD TO RESILIENCE

In prayer ask the Father to reveal any misunderstandings of Christianity that breed unrealistic expectations and disillusionment. How will this insight help with a situation you are currently facing?

_____

_____

WEEK 2

THE SEARCH FOR resilience forces us to ask what "normal Christianity" looks like. It helps us to recognize which "version" of the gospel influenced us to follow Christ and how it affects our perspectives today. Suddenly we question the jargon that first got our attention. We wonder whether we accepted Christ on His terms or just prayed "that prayer" to avoid the horrors of hell. We reckon with the meaning of a personal relationship with Christ, and we expose any misunderstandings that have made us passive in our faith. Then truth can set the record straight and make us resilient.

Read chapter 3 of *Resilient*.

Read Luke 14:28–33 and Romans 10:8–10.

REWIRED FOR RESILIENCE

Do you remember the first time someone shared the gospel with you? What was your impression of what you heard?

_____

_____

Have you ever invited someone to accept Christ? How well do you think the invitation was understood? Explain.

_____

_____

What does having a personal relationship with Christ mean to you? Has the meaning changed since reading this chapter? How?

_____

_____

What is at the crux of your relationship with Christ? Are any misunderstandings weakening the foundation of your relationship? Explain.

_____

_____

Explain where the "heaven or hell" choice fits in your salvation experience.

_____

_____

Have you inadvertently offered a soft-sell gospel? What about your presentation "softened" the truth?

_____

_____

What is wrong with formulaic Christianity? Why are formulas unnecessary?

_____

_____

Describe how we sometimes misunderstand the phrases *trusting the Lord* and *receiving the Lord.*

Resilient in the Word

How does Luke 14:28–33 help define or refine your commitment to Christ? How can Romans 10:8–10 guide your presentation of the gospel to the lost? Which other Scripture passages would help new believers form an active rather than a passive faith?

The Road to Resilience

Consider these questions: What if all of us had a greater perspective of Jesus's lordship? What if we made the gospel as simple as presenting Christ in all His beauty and splendor? What if people fell in love with Him and chose to follow Him with every iota of their energy and passion? Find the one that provokes you the most and revisit it as your week unfolds. How is your perspective changed by doing this?

WEEK 3

PASSIVITY BREEDS COMPLACENCY—a sort of multiple-choice Christianity in which the idea of imitating Christ is just one option from a spiritual menu. Complacency distorts our ideas about faith and dulls our spiritual senses. Instead of seeing Jesus as being worthy of all we are and have, He becomes in our eyes a convenient life-enhancement drug to be "taken" at our discretion. The good news is this: the light of the true gospel is the best disinfectant. We *are* called to be the resilient!

Read chapters 4 and 5 of *Resilient*.

Read Isaiah 40:9–17 and Luke 18:18–25.

REWIRED FOR RESILIENCE

Have you been scorned by other Christians? How did you react at the time? How do you see it now?

_____

_____

What is the difference between being passionate for God and feeling obligated to Him?

_____

_____

How do you respond to the treasure Christ has given you? How does your life demonstrate its value?

Inventory your top three needs and wants. What does your list reveal?

Is there any area in which you feel like a drowning man or woman? What are you desperate for? How can you address your needs more realistically?

Why is it so easy to pay attention to our preferences and so difficult to acknowledge our most fundamental needs?

Has Jesus ever been your "life-enhancement drug"? How did this approach shape your faith?

What is the real difference between following rules and following Christ?

_____

_____

RESILIENT IN THE WORD

What picture of God does Isaiah 40:9–17 paint for you? How does it influence your understanding of Luke 18:18–25?

_____

_____

THE ROAD TO RESILIENCE

Imagine yourself in Rahim's shoes. What about his testimony can help you discover resilience in your own circumstances? What specific changes does his story provoke?

_____

_____

WEEK 4

FOLLOWING CHRIST IS what Christians do. We follow Him and the example He left for us. Where He goes, we go; what He does, we do. We follow because He commanded us to do so, saying over and over in Scripture, "Follow Me." The mission could not be clearer; yet following Him is a process. We learn to do it *by doing it* and by asking His guidance as we go. The implications of following Christ are many. The sooner we know what they are, the more resilient we will become.

Read chapters 6–9 of *Resilient*.

Read John 20:27–30 and reread Romans 10:8–10.

REWIRED FOR RESILIENCE

What do you hear when Jesus says, "Follow Me"? How do these words affect your lifestyle?

_____

_____

How does following an invisible God shape your concept of Him? How does it guide your responses to Him?

_____

_____

What is the ultimate goal of following Christ? Give a specific example of how this goal influenced a recent decision you made.

_____

_____

In your own words summarize the concept of *confessing Christ*.

_____

_____

Where has "easy believism" cropped up in your life? How did you recognize it for what it was?

_____

_____

What are the telltale signs of a heart that has been captured? Which of these signs are most apparent in your walk with Christ?

_____

_____

How might you love Christ better with your emotions?

_____

_____

Have you ever mistaken *childish* faith for *childlike* faith? Explain.

_____

_____

How do your actions reveal what you believe? Has a certain action surprised you? How did it contradict what you thought you believed?

_____

_____

In what ways are you confident that Jesus is the center of your life? In which areas is the picture less clear?

_____

_____

What is our greatest need? Where does that need show up in your life? How is it filled?

_____

_____

How much of a "fish" are you? Are you immersed in the ocean of God's love? What tempts you to visit the shore?

_____

_____

RESILIENT IN THE WORD

In John 20:27–30 Jesus explained the blessing of believing without seeing. The lesson apparently impacted Thomas, who went on to accomplish great things in the kingdom. How do the same words affect you?

THE ROAD TO RESILIENCE

Without realizing it, we sometimes compartmentalize our faith, so that we follow Christ in ways that protect our comfort zones. Think about your life as a Christ follower. Honestly assess whether you have cordoned off any compartments or followed Him on your terms rather than His. What do you fear losing by surrendering all to Him?

WEEK 5

W̲E̲ ̲H̲U̲M̲A̲N̲ ̲B̲E̲I̲N̲G̲S̲ naturally want to know the meaning of things. We are prone to reasoning our way through life's challenges; in fact, we are trained to do so. This approach does not always serve us well. In matters of faith the challenge is to believe whether or not we fully understand—and *even if* the outcome is not the one we would choose. Needing to understand and control everything leaves us and our faith exposed to compromise. It is the antidote to the resilience we desire. Let's discover a better way so we can follow Him without reservation.

Read chapters 10–13 of *Resilient.*

Read Daniel 3:1–25 and John 6.

REWIRED FOR RESILIENCE

Consider the story of the three Hebrew children. What is the difference between denying your circumstances and having the faith to face them?

_____

_____

Think about your most recent prayers to God. Have you knowingly or unknowingly set any conditions with Him? Explain.

_____

_____

Do you ever feel like a "dead man or woman" walking? What holds you there? What is Christ's answer to the problem?

_____

_____

Which type of relationship listed in chapter 12 best describes the way you relate to Christ?

_____

_____

How does understanding covenant affect the way you view God and the sacrifice Jesus made for us on the cross?

_____

_____

When you feel compelled to understand or to answer the *why* questions, what are you really saying about what you believe?

_____

_____

Are you surprised to hear about the "many more" who were not healed in Oral Roberts' meetings? How does this influence your perspective going forward?

_____

_____

How might Jesus's straightforward delivery throughout John chapter 6 inform your presentation of the gospel in our twenty-first-century culture?

_____

_____

Does a miracle settle the issue? Explain your answer in terms of your own experiences.

_____

_____

Is it your job to prove Christ's claims so that people can believe? What *is* your job in presenting the gospel?

_____

_____

How does softening the gospel message impact altar calls in the short term? In the long term?

_____

_____

If God reveals something that you don't fully understand, does it impede your following Him? Why should or shouldn't it?

_____

_____

Resilient in the Word

Describe two ways in which the Hebrew children's *even if* faith was demonstrated in Daniel 3:1–25. How can their stand help you to be resilient in a current situation? How does it help you to better understand a past experience?

The Road to Resilience

Have you asked God to do a certain miracle in your life? Examine the place your request holds: is your trust invested in the miracle itself or in the God you serve? How might you adjust your perspective so that your faith is correctly placed in Him? How will this adjustment affect you going forward?

WEEK 6

S AYING YOU WANT to run a marathon and actually running it are two very different things. One is a good idea; the other is a commitment to do whatever it takes to reach the finish line. The first might give you goose bumps, but they will last only a moment. The latter will cost you something and will test your mettle over the long term. The cost is high, but don't let it scare you off. The rewards are more than all the world's wealth could buy!

Read Part 3 of *Resilient*, chapters 14–19.

Read Hebrews 12:1–2 and Hebrews 5:12–14.

REWIRED FOR RESILIENCE

What happens when you believe you are strong, but find that you cannot endure? Have you experienced this phenomenon in a particular situation? Explain.

_____

_____

What must everyone who crosses a marathon finish line submit to? How does this lesson translate to your life of faith?

_____

_____

How are muscle strength and endurance related? How are you exercising your spiritual muscles?

_____

_____

What role does pain play in your training? How does your current view of pain support or hinder your training for resilience?

_____

_____

What is the key to keeping your heart healthy, spiritually speaking? How well are you doing in this area? What improvements can you make?

_____

_____

How can you, as a follower of Christ, prepare *not* to "hit the wall"?

_____

_____

What is the surefire way to avoid spiritual junk food?

_____

_____

Competitive athletes talk about "getting inside an opponent's head." In running your spiritual race, how can you keep your own head straight?

_____

_____

What kind of "tree" are you?

_____

_____

Are your spiritual "roots" healthy enough to withstand life's storms? What are some things you can do to strengthen your roots and protect them from "pests"?

_____

_____

RESILIENT IN THE WORD

The writer of the Book of Hebrews describes the optimal spiritual diet in Hebrews 5:12–14. How do his words challenge you? If you were in Bishop Umar Mulinde's situation, how would they better position you to fulfill the mandate of Hebrews 12:1–2?

_____

_____

THE ROAD TO RESILIENCE

Success is never an accident; it always involves a commitment and a plan to fulfill the commitment. In becoming resilient what is your training plan? What practices will you implement on a regular basis in preparation for running your spiritual race to the end? What will a typical week's plan look like? (You may want to develop a spiritual workout regimen using the charts and logs in chapters 15–17.)

_____

_____

WEEK 7

J EREMIAH 17:9 SAYS, "The heart is deceitful above all things" (NKJV). Every human heart has places still needing exposure to His light. More often than we realize, we lack resilience *because* we deceive ourselves. We convince ourselves that our ways are working. We hold on to beliefs that suit our purposes and protect us from making the very changes the truth would demand. As a result, we make decisions that have painful and lasting consequences. The deserter's heart is found in all of us, but it can be exposed—and Jesus *will* heal it!

Read chapter 20 of *Resilient*.

Read Luke 15:11–24, Matthew 4:8–9, and Galatians 6:8.

REWIRED FOR RESILIENCE

For the sake of discussion, imagine how the prodigal son might have developed a deserter's heart. Develop your "story line" from what you know of human nature and your own life experiences.

What does Sergeant Charles Robert Jenkins have in common with the prodigal son? What can you learn from the similarities?

How or why do we deceive ourselves into believing that our bad choices are only about us? How does this deception make our choices even more dangerous?

_____

_____

Why does the grass seem greener on the other side? When has this illusion tripped you up? What did it cost you?

_____

_____

We know that God is a God of second chances. Explain the value of having another chance. Explain what another chance cannot give you.

_____

_____

How does humility help heal a deserting heart?

_____

_____

Have you ever elected to stay in the pigpen just a little longer? What motivated your decision?

_____

_____

RESILIENT IN THE WORD

In Matthew 4:8–9, you see Satan's deal-making approach. How and when have you been tempted to accept such a deal? How did your choice exemplify what Galatians 6:8 calls "sowing to the flesh" and "reaping from it"?

_____

_____

THE ROAD TO RESILIENCE

Think about the patterns evident in your life: lack of endurance, people-pleasing, being self-deprecating, feeling hopeless, etc. Do any of them reveal a deserting heart? Have you tried to cover up the tendency with rationales and other excuses? Will you allow Jesus to heal the deserting part of your heart? How will you make room for Him to do that?

_____

_____

WEEK 8

O UR MODEL FOR resilience is Christ. As Lion and Lamb, He is both fierce and tender; He can be fully one without compromising the other. He taught us to value the discipline of challenging situations so that we might become the relentless tribe He leads, the one He has always had in mind. This tribe has a warrior spirit that accepts pain as part of the price. It manages pain so the race is not compromised, and it leaves a legacy of resilience to undergird the generations to come. It is *your* tribe—the tribe of the resilient!

Read chapters 21–22 and the conclusion of *Resilient*.

Read 1 Peter 5:8, 2 Corinthians 4:7–9, and Matthew 6:25–33.

REWIRED FOR RESILIENCE

How does the training of the Masai warrior cut against the Western grain? In what way(s) does it line up with biblical principles?

_____

_____

How does the Maasai warrior's knowledge of his enemy's habits position him to prevail in battle? How does understanding the "impostor lion" position you to prevail in this life?

_____

_____

How does the Savior's quiet dignity encourage you to endure? How does it develop your resilience?

_____

_____

In becoming resilient, why is pain management more effective than pain avoidance?

_____

_____

Have you caught yourself chasing any "carrots"? Explain.

_____

_____

How can you relate to the story of the lottery winner? How has the very thing you desired brought you more sorrow than joy?

_____

_____

Why is it critical for us to understand how highly we are valued by Christ? How has *not* understanding this brought negative consequences?

_____

_____

You are being relentlessly pursued by Christ. How intently are you pursuing Him? What might be holding you back from pursuing Him with your whole heart?

How is your endurance important to the next generation? What legacy are you planning to leave?

Resilient in the Word

What does 2 Corinthians 4:7–9 say about the source of your resilience? How does this passage encourage you? How does it free you to become resilient?

The Road to Resilience

Matthew 6:25–33 is a powerful passage about the Christ-centered life. How can you make this passage more real in your life? What response stirs in your heart as you read it? What changes does it inspire?

NOTES

Chapter 1—Feel-Good Faith

1. One With Them, "Tamirat WoldeGorgis," http://www.onewith
-them.com/stories-of-persecution/tamirat-woldegorgis/
(accessed April 21, 2014).
2. Ibid.

Chapter 3—Passive Faith

1. A. W. Tozer, *The Pursuit of God* (Rockville, MD: Serenity Pub-
lishers, 2009), 89.
2. Blue Letter Bible, Greek Lexicon, s.v. "received" (G2983 KJV),
http://www.blueletterbible.org/lang/lexicon/lexicon
.cfm?Strongs=G2983&t=KJV (accessed April 21, 2014).

Chapter 4—The "Theology of Complacency"

1. This entire account is from Persecution.org, "Stories of the Persecuted: Perseverance of Faith in Iran," http://www.persecution
.org/crossingthebridge/tag/imprisonment/ (accessed April 23,
2014).

Chapter 5—Jesus, the Life-Enhancement Drug

1. Persecution.org, "Stories of the Persecuted: Perseverance of
Faith in Iran."
2. Ibid.
3. Ibid.

Chapter 10—Fully Alive

1. The rose on the right is the real flower.
2. Ed Payne, Catherine E. Shoichet, and Jason Hanna, "Brain-dead
Girl Jahi McMath Released From California Hospital," CNN,
January 7, 2014, http://www.cnn.com/2014/01/06/health/jahi
-mcmath-girl-brain-dead (accessed June 4, 2014).

Chapter 11—*Only If* vs. *Even If* Faith

1. ChinaAid News, "Despite Ban on Activities, Shandong House
Church Grows Since Police Raid," http://www.chinaaid
.org/2014/03/despite-ban-on-activities-shandong.html (accessed
April 24, 2014).

Chapter 12—A New Kind of Relationship

1. Tim Keller, "A Covenant Relationship," September 9, 2007, http://sermons2.redeemer.com/sermons/covenant-relationship (accessed June 3, 2014)

Chapter 14—Strength Training vs. Endurance Training

1. Morning Star News, "Young Woman in Uganda Hospitalized after Father Beats Her; Mulinde's Sight Saved," March 27, 2014, http://morningstarnews.org/2014/03/young-woman-in-uganda-hospitalized-after-father-beats-her-mulindes-sight-saved/ (accessed April 25, 2014).

Chapter 18—Focus on the Finish Line

1. Dawn González, "Dr. Ted Baehr: A Culture Warrior," ReachOut Columbia, December 2013, http://www.reachoutcolumbia.com/articles/dr-ted-baehr-a-culture-warrior/ (accessed June 24, 2014).
2. Robert D. Abrahams, "The Night They Burned Shanghai," The Intuition Mission, http://www.intuitionmission.com/fight_apathy.htm (accessed May 16, 2014); Greg Sidders, "What I Didn't Say in My Sermon," http://www.gregsidders.com/2009/08/what-i-didnt-say-in-my-sermon.html (accessed May 16, 2014).

Chapter 21—A Tale of Two Deserters

1. Jim Frederick, "In From the Cold," *Time*, December 5, 2004, http://content.time.com/time/magazine/article/0,9171,880222,00.html (accessed April 26, 2014).
2. Ibid.
3. Atika Shubert, "'Deserter' Surrenders at U.S. Base," CNN, September 11, 2004, http://www.cnn.com/2004/WORLD/asiapcf/09/11/jenkins.us/index.html?iref=newssearch (accessed April 26, 2014).
4. Graeme Wood, "The U.S. Soldier Who Defected to North Korea," *The Atlantic*, August 14, 2013, http://www.theatlantic.com/magazine/archive/2013/09/the-defector/309436/ (accessed April 26, 2014).
5. Frederick, "In From the Cold."
6. Ibid.
7. Ibid.
8. Ibid.

9. *Open Doors* (blog), "A Prayer From a North Korean Christian Just Before Going Back to His Country," March 21, 2014, http://blog.opendoorsusa.org/prayer-north-korean-christian-country/ (accessed April 28, 2014).

10. Frederick, "In From the Cold."

11. Ibid.

CHAPTER 23—THE RESILIENT ARE RELENTLESS

1. Martin Bashir and Sarah Holmberg, "Powerball Winner Says He's Cursed," ABC News, April 6, 2007, http://abcnews.go.com/2020/powerball-winner-cursed/story?id=3012631#.T3Xghr-XQto (accessed April 28, 2014); Ken Walker, "Christian Lottery Winner Stirs Furor Over Issue of Gambling," *Charisma*, http://www.charismamag.com/spirit/devotionals/loving-god?view=article&id=930:christian-lottery-winner-stirs-furor-over-issue-of-gambling&catid=154 (accessed May 18, 2014).

2. A. W. Tozer, *Mystery of the Holy Spirit* (Alachua, FL: Bridge-Logos, 2007), 14.

CONCLUSION—THIS IS OUR HERITAGE, OUR TRIBE

1. Tozer, *The Pursuit of God*, 89.

ABOUT THE AUTHOR

Ron Luce is the president and founder of Teen Mania Ministries. He passionately declares the truth of the gospel without compromise, and challenges teenagers to take a stand for Christ in their schools, communities, and throughout the world.

Raised in a broken home, Ron ran away at the age of fifteen and became involved in drug and alcohol abuse. He found Jesus at age sixteen, and the life-transforming impact of Christ inspired Ron to dedicate his life to reaching young people.

After receiving both bachelor's and master's degrees in counseling and psychology, Ron and his wife, Katie, started Teen Mania in 1986. They had nothing more than a hatchback car and a dream to raise up an army of young people who would change the world. The ministry has expanded worldwide and reaches hundreds of thousands each year with the life-transforming message of the gospel.

Ron is a sought-after expert on teen issues and the influence of pop culture. Ron speaks around the world and has authored thirty-five books helping parents and pastors understand the plight of today's youth, showing them how all of us can be part of the solution.

Recognized as a national voice on teen issues, Ron leads Acquire the Fire conferences speaking face-to-face with 3 million teens over the past twenty-seven years. Through Global Expeditions he has commissioned 74,509 teen missionaries to take the gospel around the world. Yearly hundreds of young adults spend twelve months in passionate pursuit of the Lord while building leadership skills at the university-accredited ministry internship.

Ron has appeared on CNN, *Nightline*, *Hannity*, *The O'Reilly Factor*, and in the *New York Times*, and has also made numerous media appearances on programs such as Dr. James Dobson's *Focus on the Family* radio broadcast and *The 700 Club*.

Ron and Katie live in Dallas, Texas, and have three adult children, Hannah, Charity, and Cameron.